Praise for
William Julius Wilson and Richard P. Taub's

THERE GOES THE NEIGHBORHOOD

"Both a compelling work and a disturbing one. . . . [The] assessment of a lack of common ground among different groups in the city seems spot-on." —*Time Out Chicago*

"A powerful sociological study of how the steady influx of Latinos are changing urban neighborhood dynamics and the black-white divide. A major piece of scholarship. It should be read by all those concerned with immigration and America's urban, multiethnic future."
—Lawrence D. Bobo,
Martin Luther King, Jr. Centennial Professor,
Stanford University

"An intriguing and insightful study on integration in America. . . . [Wilson and Taub's] findings provide key insights into the problems of racial and ethnic integration."
—*The Decatur Daily*

"Writing in the tradition of the 'Chicago School,' two leading students of the city show how ethnic and racial change is not an inevitable linear process. [The book shows how] white, black, and Latino working-class neighborhoods are shaped primarily by the character of local social organization and the larger context of public policy. Absorbing and thought-provoking."   —Ira Katznelson,
Ruggles Professor of Political Science and
History, Columbia University, and the author of
*When Affirmative Action Was White: An Untold History
of Racial Inequality in Twentieth-Century America*

"The conclusions remain timely."   —*Publishers Weekly*

"An important and disturbing ethnographic report on Chicago's ethnic neighborhoods that powerfully speaks to the racial divide in this country. Wilson and Taub and their innovative researchers have put their finger on the deep-seated racial attitudes that continue to divide urban America, illuminating the challenges we still face half a century after the start of the civil rights movement. This work makes important contributions to our understanding of the issues and possible solutions to the elusive goal of racial peace, comity, and mutual respect. It should be widely read."   —Elijah Anderson,
author of *Code of the Street*

William Julius Wilson
and Richard P. Taub

THERE GOES THE NEIGHBORHOOD

William Julius Wilson is the Lewis P. and Linda L. Geyser University Professor at Harvard University. He is also the author of *Power, Racism, and Privilege*; *The Declining Significance of Race*; *The Truly Disadvantaged*; and *The Bridge over the Racial Divide*. He lives in Cambridge, Massachusetts.

Richard P. Taub is the Paul Klapper Professor in the Social Sciences and Professor in the Departments of Comparative Human Development and Sociology at the University of Chicago. His previous books include *Community Capitalism* and *Paths of Neighborhood Change*.

THERE GOES THE NEIGHBORHOOD

THERE GOES THE NEIGHBORHOOD

*Racial, Ethnic, and Class Tensions in
Four Chicago Neighborhoods and
Their Meaning for America*

WILLIAM JULIUS WILSON
AND RICHARD P. TAUB

Vintage Books
A Division of Random House, Inc.
New York

FIRST VINTAGE BOOKS EDITION, OCTOBER 2007

The Library of Congress has cataloged the Knopf edition as follows:
Wilson, William J., [date]
There goes the neighborhood : racial, ethnic, and class tensions in four Chicago neighborhoods and their meaning for America / by William Julius Wilson and Richard P. Taub—1st ed.
p. cm.
Includes bibliographical references.
1. Ethnic conflict—Illinois—Chicago. 2. Chicago (Ill.)—Race relations. 3. Social conflict—Illinois—Chicago. 4. Neighborhoods—Illinois—Chicago—Case studies.
I. Taub, Richard P. II. Title.
HN80.C5W55 2006
305.8009773'11—dc22 2006041027

Vintage ISBN: 978-0-679-72418-6

Book design by Robert C. Olsson

www.vintagebooks.com

Printed in the United States of America
10 9 8 7 6 5 4

CONTENTS

ACKNOWLEDGMENTS

In the preparation of this book, we are indebted to a number of individuals and organizations. We are grateful to our editor at Knopf, Victoria Wilson, for her helpful comments on various drafts, including those that improved the flow of the manuscript. We would like to thank James Quane, who provided helpful suggestions on a previous draft. We owe a great deal to Michael Francis Maltese for his assistance in organizing the field notes and for his editorial work on an earlier draft. We are also deeply indebted to Sandra Hackman, who provided helpful editorial suggestions concerning the revision and reorganization of the final draft. We are appreciative to Susan Allen for her assistance in making the book more accessible to a general audience. We thank Brian D. Goldstein for his careful library research, Edward Walker for his careful proofreading and editing of the final draft, and Pamela Joshi for preparing the figures and tables presented in this book.

We would also like to thank the Ford Foundation, the John D. and Catherine T. MacArthur Foundation, and the Rockefeller Foundation for their support of the Center for the Study of Urban Inequality that William Julius Wilson directed at the University of Chicago during the time the collaborators, as field ethnographers, collected the data for this study. These collaborators include Erin Augis, Patrick J. Carr, Chenoa Flippen, Jennifer L. Johnson, Maria J. Kefalas, Reuben A. Buford May, Mary Pattillo, Jennifer Pashup, and Joylon Wurr. Finally, we would like to thank the Ford Foundation for their support of the Joblessness and Urban Poverty Research Program that Wilson directs at Harvard University. This support helped in the analysis and writing phase of the project.

THERE GOES THE
NEIGHBORHOOD

CHAPTER ONE

Race and Neighborhood Social Organization

T his book is an investigation into ethnic, racial, and class dynamics in four neighborhoods in Chicago, a city that has experienced a steep drop in its white population and a sharp rise in Latino residents. Chicago's Latino population grew by nearly 38 percent between 1990 and 2000, while its white population declined by almost 15 percent (see Figure 1). Whites constituted just 31 percent of the population in 2000, down from 38 percent in 1990.[1] African Americans remained Chicago's largest single group at 36 percent, but their share of the population had also dropped slightly—by 1.9 percent—after rising steadily through most of the twentieth century.

To fully capture this ethnic diversity, we felt that the most representative neighborhoods would be those that were neither poor nor affluent. We chose neighborhoods that consisted mainly of the working and lower middle classes— neighborhoods, in short, that best represented ordinary

Americans and that were more likely to be the destination of outside racial and ethnic groups seeking desirable and affordable places to live. We selected areas that were populated by

FIGURE 1. CITY OF CHICAGO: TOTAL POPULATION BY RACE AND HISPANIC ORIGIN, 1980–2000

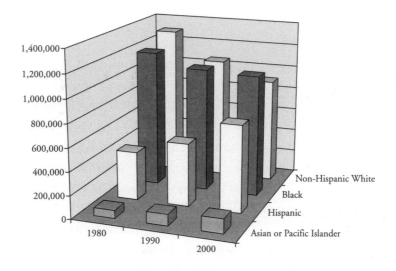

different ethnic groups to capture variations in responses to neighborhood change. In 1992, after much preliminary investigation, four were chosen—Beltway, Dover, Archer Park, and Groveland—on Chicago's South and West sides. Because some of the materials used in this study are quite sensitive, the names of these four neighborhoods are pseudonyms.[2] Beltway was chosen as the white neighborhood,

Dover as the white neighborhood in transition, Archer Park as the Latino neighborhood, and Groveland as the African American neighborhood.

The choice of neighborhoods represents what sociologist David Willer calls theoretical sampling; that is, the selection of natural cases that include the necessary conditions for the application of theoretical assumptions, assumptions that steer the research and that are used to interpret the findings.[3] The field research in this study enabled us to examine certain theoretical assumptions involving race and the social organization of neighborhoods, including Albert Hirschman's general theory of exit, voice, and loyalty— which in this instance is applied to neighborhoods.[4]

Chicago, like several major American metropolitan cities, experienced a number of intense racial eruptions in the second half of the twentieth century, as working-class whites responded angrily to the civil rights movement, proclaiming that the government's call for integrating schools and residential areas had gone too far.[5] The democratic promise of equal opportunity rang hollow for these residents, who viewed civil rights as promoting blacks at the expense of the limited financial security that working-class whites had worked hard to achieve.

These ordinary white Americans saw themselves as victims of the government's attempt to legislate a particular way of life in their homes and neighborhoods. Many white Chicago residents noted that integration did not occur at schools for the children of the wealthy and powerful, nor did the elite have to worry about declining property values. These residents also often asked why the government created policies that seemed, in their eyes, to benefit blacks alone.

For Emily Nolan, who grew up on Chicago's Southwest Side, there was no question that civil rights' time had come. But as a mother and the young wife of a Chicago police officer, she watched the battles over busing and housing engulf her neighborhood throughout the 1970s, and she resented that "outsiders" had targeted law-abiding residents of South Side neighborhoods in their efforts to bring about racial change. Nolan, watching the civil rights marchers come to the Southwest Side, remembered people saying: "Here we are keeping up our neighborhood and following the rules, living our lives. We're not hurting anyone, and these people from the University of Chicago and Martin Luther King . . . were telling us how to live our lives." She continued, "Now, I agreed with what Dr. King was saying . . . but then here were people coming to our homes and our neighborhoods telling us we had to change things."

With the threat of desegregation, white ethnic working-class neighborhoods became embattled fortresses. By the late 1970s many whites had fled these neighborhoods for the suburbs, redrawing racial boundaries as African Americans and, later, Latinos filled the resulting vacancies.

Although most white migrants moved to the suburbs, some relocated to predominantly white working-class neighborhoods on the Northwest and Southwest sides of the city. During the past two decades, Latino entry into Southwest

Side neighborhoods has further spurred white movement to other Chicago neighborhoods and to the suburbs.

This investigation was undertaken partly to better understand the factors that produced or prevented what social scientists call "the tipping point"—rapid ethnic turnover.[6] In many neighborhoods, an infusion of minorities prompted whites to leave and discouraged other whites from replacing them. Thus the proportion of minority-group members grew quickly, particularly after the minority group became a major force in the community. Real estate agents have historically abetted this process by "steering" purchasers to "live with their own kind."

Why do some neighborhoods experiencing an in-migration of outside ethic groups reach the tipping point more quickly than others, and why do other neighborhoods never reach the tipping point at all? In addressing such questions we can reflect on economist Albert Hirschman's theory of exit, voice, and loyalty, a theory that was applied to firms and organizations but that is relevant to understanding ethnic changes in neighborhoods. Hirschman argues that when people become dissatisfied with changes in their surroundings they can *exit*—move or withdraw from further participation—or they can exercise *voice*. Hirschman defines "voice" as any attempt "to change, rather than to escape from," an undesirable situation.[7]

The more willing people are to try to exercise voice—that is, to change, correct, or prevent a particular situation—the less likely they are to exit. In situations where both exit and voice options are available, past experience will largely determine whether people overcome their biases in favor of exit, the easier option. The view that a neighborhood is on the path of inexorable change, even when these changes have yet to occur, can trigger an exodus. Indeed, Americans maintain a strong bias toward the exit alternative when confronting ethnic and racial changes.

"When general conditions in a neighborhood deteriorate," writes Hirschman, "those who value most highly neighborhood qualities such as safety, cleanliness, good schools, and so forth will be the first to move out; they will search for housing in somewhat more expensive neighborhoods or in the suburbs and will be lost to the citizens' groups and community action programs that would attempt to stem and reverse the tide of deterioration."[8]

The late sociologist Hubert Blalock suggested that when minorities penetrate a neighborhood, existing residents are more likely to remain if new residents bring attractive resources such as high social status, as when in-migrants include actors, sports celebrities, or other highly prized professionals.[9] But such neighborhoods are more likely to be affluent to begin with. Minorities who move into neighborhoods populated by ordinary white citizens usually lack high-status social resources. And given that such new residents represent a larger group of people with similar occupational and educational levels and similar language skills, white residents fear that a small trickle could unleash a major invasion.

Of course, in a democratic society people are free to move.

However, as Blalock pointed out, some residents might find it too difficult or too expensive to retreat to areas where few or no minorities reside.[10] Thus, when residents view exit as problematic or costly, they are likely to turn instead to voice. Hirschman offers another explanation for why residents decide to exercise voice: the more they are loyal—that is, attached—to an organization or, in this case, a neighborhood, the less likely they are to exit. Loyalty reflects the extent to which residents are willing "to trade off the certainty of exit against the uncertainties" of improving local conditions.[11]

Loyalty becomes particularly important when it reduces the likelihood that the residents most concerned about neighborhood quality will be the first to depart. Such residents tend to be those with superior social resources and more options; they are also likely to be influential. The longer these residents stay, the less likely it is that other residents in the neighborhood will leave.

Our investigation explored to what extent—and why—residents in selected urban neighborhoods reacted to looming racial, ethnic, or class changes, and how those actions affected neighborhood stability. How residents reacted in turn reflected the dynamics of ethnic, racial, and class tensions—themselves indicative of larger forces at play.

A crucial question that we ask in this book is: To what extent are our findings consistent with the assumptions of Hirschman's theory? Our findings led us to augment his theoretical formulations—that is, to broaden the theoretical sketch and thus provide clearer direction for further research.

The neighborhoods of Beltway, Dover, and Archer Park

have one attribute in common: a growing Latino population. In 1980, Beltway—a neighborhood of some 22,000 residents featuring carefully manicured lawns and gardens dotted with statuary—was 95 percent white. However, by 2000 the white population had declined to 76 percent and the Latino population had risen to 21 percent.

Dover, with almost 45,000 residents, had experienced a remarkable ethnic transformation: in 1980, 83 percent of the population was white; in 1990, 60 percent of residents were white. However, by 2000 the white population had plummeted to 19 percent, and some 79 percent of Dover's population was Latino. Indeed, the selection of Dover provided us with the opportunity to observe intergroup tensions in a neighborhood undergoing rapid ethnic change at the time of our research.

Archer Park, a once exclusively white and largely Bohemian neighborhood, had been a Mexican enclave for several decades, and in 2000, 83 percent of the neighborhood's residents were Latino. Because its Spanish-speaking population included a high number of recent immigrants, Archer Park was poorer than the other neighborhoods (see Table 1, Appendix B). Yet even though the Mexicans who arrived in all these neighborhoods reported lower incomes, on average, than the whites they replaced, their influx shored up a sagging real estate market, and the population in these three communities grew despite white flight.

The only one of the four neighborhoods to register a population decline was Groveland, which experienced virtually no rise in its small number of Latinos, while losing almost 5 percent of its overall population since 1990. A community of close to 12,000 residents and neat single-family houses featuring trim yards, Groveland, in 2000, was 97 percent African American and featured a high percentage of long-term residents.

In scrutinizing these communities, this book documents the residents' relationships with and perceptions of other racial and ethnic groups. Surveys cannot capture nuances of behavior and attitudes, so our research relied on an ethnographic approach, using researchers trained to record subtle aspects of social and institutional behavior, including informal conversations with residents over extended periods of time (see Appendix A). We captured what sociologists call the "contextual aspects" of behavior—that is, information on the broader social environment in which the behavior occurs, including background information relevant to the behavior.

To investigate the myriad dimensions of ethnic and racial identity, we documented the extent to which the residents of each neighborhood shared modes of behavior and outlook, including values, preferences, aspirations, and worldviews.[12] We also observed how residents defined and handled collective problems, and to what extent they organized to maintain effective social control—for example, curbing deviance in public spaces, keeping out undesirable populations, channeling public resources toward local collective goals, and so on. The purpose here was to collect data on neighborhood social organization, defined as the extent to which the residents of a neighborhood are able to maintain effective social control and realize their collective goals.[13]

Effective neighborhood social organization depends on residents who collectively supervise community activities, take responsibility for addressing problems, and actively participate in voluntary and formal organizations, including parent-teacher organizations, civic and business groups, block clubs, churches, and political groups.[14]

Our ethnographic team consisted of nine graduate-student research assistants at the University of Chicago who immersed themselves in these neighborhoods for almost three years, from January 1993 to September 1995. Three of the research assistants covered Archer Park, while two conducted research in each of the three communities of Beltway, Dover, and Groveland. The races of the investigators matched those of the neighborhoods: African American graduate students carried out field research in Groveland; white graduate students covered Beltway. Although whites conducted the ethnographic research in Dover and Archer Park, which included substantial numbers of Latino residents, all five of these graduate students spoke at least some Spanish, and two of the three field-workers in Archer Park were fluent in Spanish.

The study of racial, ethnic, and class tensions in four Chicago neighborhoods has implications for the future of the country as a whole. In the latter half of the 1990s the United States enjoyed an incredible economic boom that lessened social tensions across the nation. During that period crime and poverty were reduced and the fiscal condition in many cities improved significantly.[15] However, the recession of 2001, followed by a jobless recovery, undermined this brief period of economic progress.

Furthermore, the Bush administration's sharp cuts in federal aid to states aggravated the problems of providing basic services, including public education, in central cities dependent on state funds.[16] And the huge tax cuts, the war in Iraq, and the war against terrorism have further siphoned off monies that could be used to address social problems in urban areas, including inner-city neighborhoods. The combined result of these political and economic changes is that many central cities and inner suburbs are left with vast concentrations of poverty, "without the fiscal capacity to grapple with the consequences: joblessness, family fragmentation, and failing schools."[17]

Many financially secure urban residents are therefore encouraged to move to the suburbs, and those who remain find themselves competing along racial and ethnic lines for limited resources, including housing, desirable neighborhoods, schools, parks, and playgrounds. These actions give rise to decisions that affect neighborhood stability and racial and ethnic tensions, and these decisions are played out in various ways among the neighborhoods featured in this study.

Given the diminished federal and state resources, it is important to be familiar with the forces at work in urban neighborhoods, to understand why people react the way they do, and to address a major national challenge: the development of intergroup harmony in an era of rapid ethnic change.

CHAPTER TWO

Beltway

A Predominantly White Community
at the City's Edge

————

Written with the collaboration of
Patrick J. Carr and Maria J. Kefalas

W hen Chicago experienced racial turmoil beginning in the 1960s, many whites who remained in the city relocated to working-class neighborhoods on the Northwest and Southwest sides. Beltway was the destination of many of these whites who arrived from communities undergoing racial and ethnic turnover, such as Dover, Archer Park, Marquette Park, and Bridgeport. Some residents moved to Beltway because the 1960s highway-building boom had dissected their previous neighborhoods, while others sought larger, newer homes for growing families.

Of the four communities investigated in this book, Beltway is the farthest from downtown Chicago and the most isolated, wedged between Midway Airport and the city limits. Residents generally felt that these de facto boundaries provided them with a clearly demarcated physical space that was "their" neighborhood. Given the proximity of communities with high concentrations of poverty and crime, Beltway residents took pride in the fact that people did not immediately recognize their neighborhood as part of the city. They joked about how visitors often asked, "Is this still Chicago?" A former president of the Beltway Civic League noted that Beltway was "not chaotic. The population isn't on top of you. It's not high density and still residential . . . People in a lot of ways are isolated out here, and part of that they want and like."

Chicago law requires that city employees live inside the city limits, so Beltway became an attractive residential option for white municipal employees. Community residents expressed pride in the disproportionately high number of Chicago police officers and firefighters who lived in Beltway, and tended to hold the view that the neighborhood was more stable and secure because of these municipal employees.[1] Indeed, among our four communities, Beltway's residential stability was second only to Groveland's, with 62 percent of residents reporting in 2000 that they had lived in the same home for five years or more.

For white blue-collar and service workers in Chicago— police officers, firefighters, streets and sanitation workers, and park district employees—Beltway was an appealing community. The housing was affordable, the neighborhood was relatively safe, the quality of city services was high, and the residents felt that Beltway was one of the last places where white, working-class Chicagoans could live among people whom they felt shared their backgrounds, experiences, and values.

As other urban communities became increasingly rootless and atomized in the wake of suburbanization, demographic shifts, and deindustrialization, the residents of Beltway struggled to maintain their distinctive way of life, and this vigilance strengthened residents' ties to one another and to the community.[2] Beltwayites generally knew their neighbors and regularly discussed the neighborhood's "small-town" feel, commenting, "Everybody knows what everybody else is doing." Some even complained that their neighbors' interest could be intrusive.

On warm summer days, Beltway families sat outside on their porches watching their children and chatting with neighbors. Summer brought several church festivals, a picnic at the Garland School, block parties, and parades. Nearby Pond Meadows Park and Garland Park both offered day camps for local children. Amid what was becoming "a nation of strangers," Beltway residents still honored the community, maintaining it with the same care they lavished on their cars. "I think that people who live here like it," said Laura Davis, who has lived in Beltway for thirty-five years. "They come here planning to stay. They don't [come] planning to leave. There are some neighborhoods where people buy a house because this is a step on the ladder. And as soon as they can afford it, they're going to move to a better house or a better neighborhood. This is not the greatest neighborhood in the world, but people feel at home here, and they don't move."

Despite Beltway's apparently high level of stability, comfort, and interaction, residents glorified a past—a time before air conditioners and television—when people were even more likely to interact with their neighbors. Racial and class homogeneity characterized much of Beltway's history. Beltway was 95 percent white in 1980 (see Figure 2). A decade later, the percentage of whites had fallen only slightly as the Latino population—mainly Mexican Americans—rose to 7.5 percent. However, signs were appearing that the neighborhood, once a white fortress, was beginning a process of significant change. The white population declined by almost 14 percent between 1990 and 2000, while the Latino population swelled to 21 percent. Whites composed only 76 percent of Beltway's population. Unlike in Dover or Archer Park, the majority of Beltway's growing Latino population was second- or third-generation American, so these residents were more affluent and better educated than were recent Spanish-speaking immigrants, and well assimilated to U.S. social and economic customs. One Latino police officer who lived and worked in Beltway gently corrected one of our field-workers when she pronounced his name with a Spanish accent. In a thick Chicago accent, he explained, "It's Vil-la-ree-awl," not "Vee-uh-ree-awl."

Until 1990, only a handful of African Americans lived in Beltway, but by 2000 the number of African American residents there had grown to nearly 300. Although blacks continued to represent less than 1 percent of the population, the fact that they were beginning to penetrate the neighborhood was symbolic.

Many Beltway residents felt they had been driven to the edges of the city by minorities. They noted that neighborhoods such as Beltway—"urban versions of the 'little republics' that Thomas Jefferson" envisioned as "democracy's local outposts"—were once common.[3] Now, however, white residents perceived such neighborhoods as an endangered species.

FIGURE 2. BELTWAY: TOTAL POPULATION BY RACE AND HISPANIC ORIGIN, 1980–2000

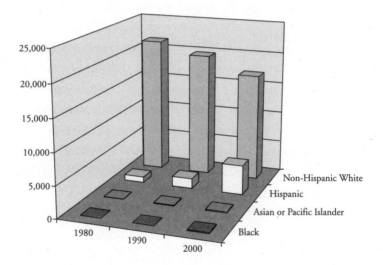

After the racially charged upheavals of the 1960s and the ensuing social, economic, and demographic shifts, Chicago became less recognizable for working-class whites. As Colleen Sampson, a longtime Beltway resident and community activist, explained, "What you have to understand is that for many people they have had to move once or twice . . . and for them Beltway is the last stand . . . When Martin Luther King marched on Chicago, he went to places like Marquette Park and so on. People in places like Gage Park, you know . . . just left. So, many people who live here had to move once or twice."

Thomas Clifton, a seventy-year-old Beltway resident and business owner, similarly noted, "We have the Blue Hill area, we have this area, we have Chelsea up on the Northwest Side. That's all that's left of Chicago that romantics like myself may seek. I'm afraid to say that is why an awful lot of people have moved here. It's just for that reason that we have an awful lot of city workers here."

Younger as well as older residents accepted this "last-stand" image of Beltway. As Terrie Johnson, a Chicago police officer in her thirties and a former Dover resident, explained, "My husband and I are both city workers and we're raising our kids here, and I don't know about you, but we ain't going nowhere." Alicia Connell, a twenty-five-year-old Beltway resident, mother of four, business owner, community activist, wife of a Chicago police officer, and former candidate for alderman, pointed out, "Beltway has been referred to as the last garden spot in Chicago. Basically, it has been fortified as that kind of community. The property values are soaring. City workers are still moving in."

For Beltway residents, the arrival of people of color was inextricably linked with poverty, crime, disorder, and decay. These residents saw the neighborhood's boundaries as separating them from the forces of social and economic depravity that they felt could destroy the fabric of their community. Residents had watched area neighborhoods change from white ethnic strongholds into communities with very different racial compositions, and noted that with these transformations came growing crime rates and social disorganization, along with declining social institutions and property values.

Asked about white homeowners' views of Beltway's changing racial makeup, Matthew Walker, a high school vice principal, replied, "Sure they fear it. As a practical issue, they fear the loss of value to their property." And a local alderman commented on the influx of people of color:

> Oh, yeah, racially it's changed, and I don't want to say the community is racist. I say the community is very conservative, and they're very concerned about their homes, their schools, and their property values, and they want to be able to walk the streets safely, they want to improve on their homes if they're going to live here for the rest of their lives. They don't want their area to "go under," so to speak, like . . . certain areas in the other parts of the city.

Beltway citizens generally viewed the arrival of even a few minorities as a threat to their well-being. John Adamski, a former Chicago alderman, explained the appeal of Beltway to white, working-class Chicagoans:

> This area on the Southwest Side of the city and [the area on] the Northwest Side of the city of Chicago are really

the last two, how shall I say, bastions of neighborhood stability, so to speak . . . What is happening, though, is that people who work for the city of Chicago have to live in the city, so I'm getting a lot of younger people, policeman, firemen [*pause*] who have lived in the city, moving to the Southwest Side . . . They move for whatever reason. There're areas of the city with high crime rates or the neighborhoods are changing, so to speak, and people start moving either to the Southwest Side or Northwest Side if they have to remain in the city.

Working-class whites in Beltway who fled their former neighborhoods tended to consider themselves victims of social transformations beyond their control. One woman reflected on problems in her former neighborhood, now a Latino enclave:

Last Christmas, I went to visit some friends who still live in [Archer Park] . . . I actually cried when I went there. There was trash on the street. Why would people leave a dirty, used diaper on the street? When I was growing up in [Archer Park], I had to go out and scrub down the stoop when the weather permitted; there were horses and men and we still managed to keep things clean.

Beltwayites felt that whites in Chicago had lost many of the racial battles over neighborhoods, especially those involving local schools. Because students from black and Latino neighborhoods were bused into schools in Beltway, neighborhood schools provided a forum for discussing race. Community leaders often publicly proclaimed that busing and "the blacks" had caused the decline of the neighborhood school, and they felt that in the aftermath of school desegregation battles, Fredrick Lee High School and public schools throughout Chicago had suffered immensely. According to Matthew Walker, vice principal of Fredrick Lee, which served Beltway and surrounding areas:

> There was a lot of violence here; school was closed prematurely. I can't remember if it was '74 or '75. There were riots or whatever word you want to put on it, outside the building and in the corridors, and it was incredible mayhem. Police had to come and spend a week here, in the corridors with helmets on, and school was closed a week early for the safety of all concerned. Well, that never left, that memory is vivid today—that is all attributed to "them" although many of the players were white . . . I had a graduate who I thought was an average, decent human being stop me in the bank over here at the end of the block a couple years ago and say to me: "When are you gonna get them out of our neighborhood?"

As Walker noted, the fact that "many of the players were white" was lost on most residents. Although episodes of racial violence in the schools had subsided by the time of our study, the busing of people of color into the neighborhood remained at the forefront of concerns among Beltway's white residents. They feared that minorities from other districts cared little about neighborhood facilities and were more likely to commit acts of vandalism on school grounds.

Beltwayites recognized that the enduring effects of the civil rights movement made it difficult to control the racial makeup of their schools, their workplaces, and even their neighborhoods. Beltway residents commonly recalled a time when jobs were plentiful and neighborhoods seemed safer. According to them, this golden era ended abruptly when the civil rights movement gave people of color greater access to resources and power. In settings such as the corner bar or the kitchen table, Beltwayites expressed racial hostility when explaining fears about crime, economic uncertainty, and neighborhood instability.

The views of Mark Alcott, an electrician for the city park district who lived in Beltway, illustrated a common belief— although couched in unusually extreme language—that working-class whites were better off when the system guaranteed them better jobs and neighborhoods. Alcott's animus toward "the niggers and minorities" revealed his fears about job security and his belief that blue-collar jobs "used to be for life" and had once been enough to "raise a family":

> The whole park district is fucked anyway. They're talking about bringing in contractors to do our jobs . . . This whole city is going down the fucking toilet . . . If [Mayor Daley's] dad knew what he was doing he would turn in his grave. Now old man Daley, he was for the blue-collar worker. Used to be that when you had those jobs you had

'em for life and you could raise a family. It's all different now, taxes and all that shit is killing the workingman. We're paying to support all the fucking niggers and minorities . . . Yeah, but I'll tell ya, if this city keeps going the way it is, it's gonna drive all the good working people right out of it. It's all fucked up and I tell ya why: too many niggers an' Mexicans an' minorities in this city. I mean niggers don't pay taxes, spics don't pay taxes. If we leave there'll be nothing in this goddamn city.

Reflecting on such views, Mary, a local librarian, maintained: "People around here don't believe that there is such a thing as a black middle-class person. I mean people around here would be shocked to learn that they would be considered 'white trash' by some of the brothers."

Many Beltwayites believed that the government gave preferential treatment not only to racial and ethnic minorities but to foreigners as well. Beltwayites talked constantly about how they paid taxes, yet racial minorities and immigrants received a disproportionately high share of welfare, food stamps, and Medicaid. For example, in a letter to the editor in the local newspaper in March 1996, a Beltway resident argued that immigrants and foreigners have "never paid a dime in taxes" and "show no respect for our laws or the American people":

Americans born and raised here better wake up! You too have been the people paying your taxes all your life in this country. Too bad many of you or most of you are not entitled to the same benefits as many of the immigrants who never paid a dime in taxes. If they accept benefits from our country, then they should start respecting it mostly by speaking the English language. I feel it's an insult to the American people born here that a foreigner speaks in a foreign tongue in public. Talk at home if you want to, but in public keep it in English. Secondly, I am sure that our retired Americans on fixed incomes could use food stamps and medical aid, [but] since they are born here, they can't get this help. Americans born here should be equal to the same rights and benefits as foreigners. It seems as if Americans are losing control of their country. Thirdly, the foreigners don't seem to have the same respect for our laws or the American people. So wake up America. Charity begins at home. Let's start helping Americans and our own people first.

Similarly, during a meeting on community policing, residents complained that the same number of officers who worked in Beltway patrolled a poorer, nonwhite neighborhood, even though it was considerably smaller. A woman in her thirties asked, "How could we get more police coverage on this beat?" A black police officer smiled and responded in a joking but tactless manner, "How about if we double your taxes and hire more police officers?" His comment struck a painful chord: one woman in the back of the room spoke up, saying, "Well, we're the only ones paying our taxes!" Other residents concurred, complaining about the taxes they already paid. One woman spoke bitterly about how she moved from "the east," where she paid a lower property tax but received better police coverage. Another woman added, "You know the people in Cabrini-Green [an overwhelmingly black public housing project] don't pay taxes." The complaints swelled into an uproar as residents expressed their dissatisfaction with the community's police presence, especially compared with smaller areas in "the east."

Some older residents displayed xenophobic attitudes in their remarks on race and Beltway's changing demographics—assuming, for example, that new Latino residents were undocumented immigrants. Other residents were concerned that teens bused to Fredrick Lee High School from poorer neighborhoods surrounding Beltway would get a preview of the area and try to move in after graduating. Implicit in these remarks was a concern that an influx of nonwhites would "ghettoize" the neighborhood. At a school-council meeting, for example, one audience member expressed her concern over the presence of minorities at a Beltway basketball facility: "I've lived out here for forty-six years in [Sampson Park]. And it isn't even warm yet and they are taking over . . . They're coming here from other neighborhoods. They're niggers coming here to play basketball."

It became obvious that race dialogue in Beltway often lacked the constraints of political correctness. At a soccer practice in the park, individuals told racist jokes to our investigators, such as: "What is black and yellow and a happy sight? A busload of black guys going over a cliff." And at local police meetings and school-council meetings, some residents, generally older, routinely used the word "nigger" to describe blacks from neighboring areas. No residents showed obvious discomfort with this use of racially charged invectives.

SOCIAL ORGANIZATION AND CONCERNS ABOUT RACE

In Beltway, the residents' impressive network of dense acquaintanceships; extended families; residential stability; common ethnic, racial, and class background; and strong institutional ties provided the community with a solid foundation for vibrant social organization. In turn, efforts to achieve many common goals—including maintaining relative stability in the neighborhood's racial mix—reflected the community's high level of social control, which itself drew strength from a shared set of social values.

Of ten active community organizations in Beltway, nine focused on maintaining "community quality." These included the Beltway Civic League (BCL), the Garland Parents Alliance (GPA), the Midway Airport Business Association, park advisory councils, church boards, and four local school councils. Beltway's two aldermen worked closely with Mayor Richard M. Daley. However, the issues that were pursued often reflected the fact that racial antagonisms varied by age.

Although both younger and older Beltwayites exhibited race prejudice, younger residents, who had not witnessed the struggles over busing and desegregation during the sixties and seventies, possessed a different perspective on race. Two community organizations, the BCL and the GPA, clearly illustrated this generational divide.

Older residents who moved to the area in the fifties and early sixties dominated BCL, an organization that had existed for four decades. BCL's members had been young parents and new homeowners during the civil rights era. Most witnessed, in some cases firsthand, Martin Luther King's marches on white ethnic strongholds such as Marquette Park and Gage Park. In fact, during the 1960s, BCL activists had become involved in the racially charged battles over fair housing, busing, and desegregation. At a public hearing on fair housing legislation in June 1967, Jennifer Powell, a former Beltway resident who was then active with the BCL, expressed sentiments that still resonate today with many Beltway residents of her generation: "I said we would not accept such legislation, even if the Supreme Court approved it . . . People want to live among their own kind, and any occupancy law, if passed, will not help to 'love thy neighbor.' "

Even though our researchers felt that most BCL members would probably have agreed with Powell that "people want to live among their own kind," they knew they could not express such sentiments without being branded racists. BCL activists focused instead on maintaining the status quo. For example, with the support of Beltway aldermen, the organization opposed the city's new mortgage program, which allowed Chicago residents to apply for low-interest loans and assistance with down payments to purchase property in the city.

Proponents of the program maintained that it would buoy housing demand and stabilize neighborhoods. However, the BCL feared that the program would destabilize property values and create a foothold for lower-income people of color. On one occasion, the BCL president read a letter from the city that, in his view, "was filled with double-talk." He then stated emphatically, "[The city] says this mortgage program is supposed to stabilize the ward! This ward is already stabilized!" Despite harsh criticism that their opposition was racially motivated, Beltway aldermen also vociferously opposed the mortgage subsidy program before the city council. In response to critics, one alderman insisted that he was simply representing the views of his constituents.

The BCL was representative of the way many residents addressed racial interaction. However, although some argued that racist sentiment in Beltway was pervasive, many younger Beltwayites who attended school and encountered people of color in social venues exhibited more liberal views. While older residents insulated themselves from people of color by remaining within the sphere of all-white neighborhood institutions, younger residents were more likely to work in integrated settings, particularly in municipal jobs. They also had children in public schools, which included nonwhite parents, students, and teachers.

Younger Beltwayites interacted with nonwhite instructors and administrators regularly, and parents of various races had to work together to influence school policies. Such alliance building occurred around governance at the Garland School. For years, two families and their close friends effectively ran the local school council (LSC) at Garland.[4] Frustrated parents who felt that the LSC ignored their opinions formed a group called the Garland Parents Alliance (GPA). This coalition concerned itself with all children who attended Garland and strove to make the LSC more accountable to residents. One of the most active members of GPA, and a candidate for the LSC, spoke about her personal volunteer efforts:

> I used to volunteer at a school in [the neighborhood] where we used to live, and I'd see some of the kids comin' into school and they would have one pair of sneakers, falling apart in the winter, no proper winter coats. I would go out and buy them a coat. My husband says that I would have spent all my money on them. I suppose I would, but it just breaks my heart to see kids like that . . . That's why I spend all this time at the school, you have to help in whatever way you can . . . Like [the family that runs the LSC], they won't let parents participate, so what is it all for? It's supposed to be about the kids, that's all we wanna do is help out the kids.

In trying to break the monopoly on power enjoyed by the LSC, GPA parents enlisted the support of teachers and administrators from the Chicago Board of Education. They also approached nonwhite parents from nearby neighborhoods, whose children were bused to Garland, to secure votes against LSC policies. These younger white Beltwayites seemed to have no difficulty working with African American administrators assigned by the Board of Education to address LSC accountability. In fact, many white residents gave one black school official particularly high marks for the way she dealt with the LSC.

Even though the group that led the opposition to the LSC was mostly white, a number of parents from Latino and black families played key roles in the efforts to overcome the LSC's monopoly. For instance, on council election day, one Latino father, a Chicago firefighter, took the day off to work with the GPA campaign. While distributing leaflets, he and another Spanish-speaking parent approached Latino parents and encouraged them to vote for the GPA-supported slate of candidates. Sitting in the kitchen of one of Beltway's white GPA members, our field-worker met a number of people who were involved in the Garland reform movement, one of whom took special care to mention the accomplishments of the firefighter.

This reform effort was conducive to uniting the whites, Latinos, and blacks because the participants shared a common concern—the education of their children. However, not all Beltwayites, particularly older residents, found themselves in collaborative situations, so their stereotypical views remained unchallenged by experience. And these views were reflected in the social organization of Beltway.

SOCIAL ORGANIZATION
AND A RACIAL BELIEF SYSTEM

White lower-middle-class culture emphasizes the family, the church, and the neighborhood, as the late historian Christopher Lasch has shown. Residents value community more than individual advancement, social solidarity more than mobility, and maintenance of existing ways over conventional ideals of success. Parents want their children to do well, but they also want them to defer to their elders, to take responsibility for their actions, and to show courage under adversity. "More concerned with honor than with worldly ambition," these parents, according to Lasch, "have less interest in the future than do upper-middle-class parents, who try to equip their children with the qualities for competitive advancement."[5]

If concerns about the family, the church, and the neighborhood are typical of white lower-middle-class culture, they were even more pronounced in Beltway because residents integrated them into a common belief system viewed as crucial for preserving the neighborhood. Beltwayites' social organization benefited from this belief system, shared by residents of all ages, which emphasized the importance of social conservatism, patriotism, and an adherence to neighborhood standards, including a commitment to keeping up the neighborhood, maintaining order, and sustaining the quality of public services. Daily discourse among residents emphasized these core components, which were interrelated in the eyes of Beltwayites. The net effect was clear norms for proper behavior, including immediately removing graffiti and prohibiting children from roaming the streets unsupervised.

The emphasis on preserving property values and maintaining order reflected the fear that an influx of minorities could drastically undermine the ideals that residents had fought so hard to uphold. Being "from Beltway" carried special meaning for residents, which in turn helped shape and crystallize local sentiments, including the common belief system.

Beltwayites had experienced the social transformation of urban America with a mixture of consternation, uncertainty, and indignation, and they prominently subscribed to the nationwide working-class backlash against social and political movements originating in the 1960s, such as affirmative action, gay rights, and feminism.[6] When conservative religious leaders such as Jerry Falwell and Pat Robertson attacked these social and cultural movements as the source of America's decline, their views resonated with Beltwayites. As former alderman John Adamski explained:

> The Beltway community is . . . white, ethnic, a serving community. A lot of blue-collar workers, a lot of people who have worked hard to buy their homes, who have worked hard to put their kids through school. It's a very conservative, roll-up-the-sleeves type of community. They work hard: not so many people out here were born with silver spoons. Most of the people have worked for what they have and I think that has a lot to do with how people take pride in their property, take pride in their schools, just have that work ethic, that pride in the neighborhood.

Holidays like Veterans Day and the Fourth of July and military anniversaries such as D-Day were important occasions in Beltway. Flags flew from houses throughout the neighborhood on these holidays, and local officials sponsored several parades each year. Festivities even included an All-American Girl contest. The military continued to be an honored career path, and the local newspaper proudly notified the public whenever a young person from the neighborhood joined the armed forces. Appreciation of military service reflected the fact that many Beltway residents had fought in World War II, Korea, and Vietnam. Veterans often talked about their experiences in Vietnam, and many residents were actively involved in POW/MIA groups. The Beltway Civic League lobbied the U.S. Postal Service for a stamp commemorating POWs and MIAs,[7] and the Beltway library often displayed memorabilia from local veterans and mounted a display in honor of POWs.

For Beltway residents, patriotism entailed more than veneration of military service. At the beginning of every public meeting—including those of the BCL and the local school council—everyone stood and faced the flag, hands over hearts, and recited the Pledge of Allegiance. When the BCL celebrated its thirty-fifth anniversary at Antonio's Italian restaurant, the function room did not include a flag. Without missing a beat, John Szymanski, president of the BCL, designated a place on the wall for an imaginary flag, and everyone solemnly recited the pledge facing the bare wall. Even the children at the summer program at Pond Meadows Park said the pledge every morning.

Patriotism also encompassed an overarching respect for "the American way of life," including an appreciation of freedom and support for U.S. industries. At public meetings, American automobiles packed the parking lots; on a number of occasions, the only foreign car in view was one field researcher's Toyota. Patriotism was not a passive ideology; residents often identified it as the basis for neighborhood activism, including efforts to resist change.

For example, two of the six candidates in the aldermanic election of 1995 prominently invoked their military service and patriotism to indicate their suitability for public office. One candidate further invoked "the American way of life" when expressing concern about maintaining the "integrity of the neighborhood"—a euphemism for opposing racial change: "We have to keep the integrity of our neighborhoods, and our American way of life. The answer lies in the past; the principles and morals that we had, we have to bring them back. I am on the Security Committee of the Regional Community Congress, I am a U.S. Army veteran, so I have experience and ideas to be alderman."

When Beltwayites spoke of bringing back the "principles and morals" of an earlier era, they were referring to the period when white neighborhoods were stable and racially homogenous and no one challenged the system of residential segregation. Efforts to maintain the neighborhood's social organization—including sanctions on those who violated community norms—helped residents resist powerful and threatening forces of change.

According to residents, the social transformation of white neighborhoods was one consequence of these powerful forces of change. In the eyes of some community members, a white neighborhood undergoing change was a neighborhood in decline. As the neighborhood's fabric weakened, it became vulnerable to penetration by outside groups. Signs that a neighborhood was "going down" included the appearance of empty lots, graffiti, poorly maintained lawns, large numbers of FOR SALE signs, and unsupervised young people. Residents linked these attributes to crime, gangs, and social decay.[8]

Beltwayites sensed that the stability of their neighborhood was fragile and that they had to anticipate and defeat negative forces. People generally believed that without constant monitoring, decay could irrevocably ruin an area.

For many residents, Beltway was the first place they had owned a home, which symbolized a lifetime of hard work and sacrifice,[9] and Beltway residents often described their neighbors as "house proud." Indeed, while the bungalows that lined Beltway's streets were quite ordinary, one could not help but notice the neatness of the homes and the often elaborately landscaped lawns. Many Beltway residents decorated their yards, porches, and windows with displays for the holidays and other special events, such as when the Chicago White Sox competed in the play-offs. In an interview during a Chicago heat wave that produced record temperatures, Laura Davis attested:

And I'd walk to [Winston] and I'd see everybody's lawn. And there are more "house proud" people out here than I've ever seen. You can really tell. Some blocks, I mean every lawn is perfect. You don't see too many where they just let it go . . . I mean we've got people down the street [who] get down on their hands and knees with a pair of scissors. To do stuff like that takes time. But nobody seems to just let it go. They care maybe about what the neighbors think of them.

To the outside observer, upkeep of property would seem to represent simply pride in homeownership and a commitment to the beauty of a neighborhood—an emphasis shared in working-class communities throughout the country. However, clean property also reinforced the notion that Beltway was "the last remaining garden spot," and that people were determined to keep it that way.

Heightened concerns about graffiti demonstrated the link between property deterioration and fear of change. Residents of some of Chicago's neighborhoods may view "taggers"— those who mark buildings with gang symbols—as a minor irritation and graffiti as merely the foul play of mischievous adolescents. However, Beltway residents viewed the defacement of public buildings as an assault on community values. Longtime resident Colleen Sampson explained that the neighborhood's biggest problems were disaffected teenagers and graffiti: "Our area gang is the Insane Popes. I think that when a neighborhood loses the graffiti fight there is a whole change in the neighborhood and what is perceived to be a safe neighborhood. I really don't want to see that change out here."

An off-duty police officer who lived in Beltway recounted how he felt upon capturing a local boy from the neighborhood who was tagging a public school building: "I mean it's bad enough doing something like that, but in your own neighborhood for Christ's sake. Like when I caught him and his father comes to the scene, I'm looking at the father and I'm thinking, 'I see this guy pass my house everyday. Who would do something that stupid?' "

John Fitzgerald, director of the Catholic Union, explained the link between crime, graffiti, and perceived change in Beltway:

> Crime is the biggest problem facing the community. Crime in this neighborhood is not as apparent as in other parts of the city. Gang crime is crawling into these neighborhoods so slowly that it is insidious. It starts with the graffiti and then [the kids] hanging out . . . Graffiti is a focal point in the community's anxiety about crime. We don't want the taggers to have a moment of glory. We want to make taggers work. And we don't want folks to give up.

Several residents aggressively pursued a Latino youth who tagged one of the neighborhood's schools with graffiti. By attending hearings and pressuring judges, they forced a full-fledged trial, which resulted in a conviction. The court sentenced the perpetrator to serve a hundred hours of community service and to pay a large fine to repair the damage. According to one resident, "We showed them that we won't take any of that shit . . . If you didn't go after those punks, well then you're saying you have just given up." To counter such trends, a number of Beltwayites participated in the mayor's Graffiti Busters Program, joined neighborhood watches, and volunteered for parent patrols at area schools.

Given their worries about keeping the neighborhood stable, the supervision of children was a growing concern of Beltway residents. They often expressed fear of young people who run wild, lack adult supervision, and seem to reject authority—especially that wielded by parents, teachers, and the police. Many residents recalled a time when community members were more willing to supervise or discipline other people's children. Today, they said, fears of gang violence and the prevalence of guns dissuaded most adults, especially the elderly, from intervening in situations involving young people.

The overriding general concern was that young people bred disorder. Growing intra-neighborhood gang violence showed that outsiders were not the sole perpetrators of youthful crime. The shooting deaths in December 1995 of two local thirteen-year-old girls caught in crossfire between Beltway's white gang members shocked the community and heightened concerns about the need to control young people. Six Beltway teenagers, including a Chicago police officer's son, were charged with murder.

Residents constantly implored local police to be more aggressive with wayward youth, and parents worked assiduously to ensure that schools adequately punished students who violated policies. Beltwayites expressed little sympathy for the difficulties facing young people, often recalling the tribulations of their own early lives.

Residents aired such sentiments at a meeting of the BCL, where police officer Richard Bonner discussed youth gangs operating in the area and indicated that crime was on the rise as a result. Following his comments, some of the BCL members spoke in disparaging terms about young people. The room erupted with demands for aggressive and preemptive actions to stave off criminal activity.[10]

Suddenly, amid the chaos of distraught citizens, Peter Ridge, the new president of the BCL, rose to his feet. A slender ten-year-old boy named Eric McLure sat patiently by his side. Eric, who represented the Boy Scouts of America, had attended the meeting at Ridge's invitation to tell the BCL about a graffiti-cleanup program he and his peers were pursuing as a community service. Eric hoped that he could gain sponsorship from the BCL for his enrollment in a Boy Scout summer camp. Ridge quieted the membership and introduced Eric by saying:

> I wasn't planning to do this now. But I have a young man here with me today, Eric McLure, who is a good kid. He is a scout. And I brought him here today because he wants the Civic League to sponsor him for twenty hours of community service so that he can go to summer camp. His community service will be to identify the graffiti in the neighborhood so we can get the city to clean it up and to help me with the tire drive. I want to know if the league will sponsor him.

Just as the crowd quieted, Officer Bonner loudly declared: "These kids [*indicating Eric*] are very sophisticated about the gangs. Your kids can be shot just [for] wearing the wrong colors. You see these kids wearing the sports jackets, like Michigan . . . They don't know anybody on the teams. These kids are really sophisticated about the gangs."

Officer Bonner called upon the boy to identify the gangs in Beltway, and their colors, and Eric nervously answered, "The Kings are red and black and the Two-Sixers have crosses, and I don't remember the rest of them." The officer persisted, maintaining, "[Eric] isn't telling us as much as he knows. But again, just to show you how much these kids know . . . Tell me which gang just tagged all around Leahy Park." Eric's response confirmed Officer Bonner's suspicion: "The Kings just tagged the building."

Suddenly, by virtue of his casual knowledge of gang activity, Eric became a symbol for all that was wrong in Beltway and society in general in the eyes of many league members, and the response was vociferous. To dampen the uproar, Officer Bonner held that "We need some backing from the community." However, the group remained tense, especially since some BCL members misunderstood Eric to be a gang member. Leila Catan then asked the frightened ten-year old boy to stand up:

LEILA CATAN: You are a Boy Scout?

ERIC MCLURE: Yes.

LEILA CATAN: Do you know the oath of the Boy
   Scouts?

ERIC MCLURE: To try to do your best [people at the
   meeting are whispering among themselves, "He
   doesn't know it"] . . . to love your country . . .

LEILA CATAN: Then why are you in a gang?

Once again attendees clamored, and Ridge tried to calm everyone by explaining that Eric was not a gang member. With the room again quiet, Catan retracted her statements, though she did not apologize to Eric for upsetting him. One woman remarked to our field researcher that the boy must have felt frightened by this band of self-righteous inquisitors. The BCL eventually voted to give Eric the money for the camp—although it did not extend apologies to the boy— and then Officer Bonner distributed leaflets explaining how to identify gang members.

While this example may appear extreme, it was in fact typical of many involving Beltway's older residents. Resident Colleen Sampson explained that tense relations were part of a generation gap exacerbated by public meetings that foment misconceptions about youngsters:

> I suppose that there is a bit of a gap between the BCL people and the young people, but I don't think that it's always the parents' fault. Someone should consult us sometimes because I think that we are misunderstood too. I think that the young people should get to go to these meetings because they are not all gangbangers, but some people don't see it that way; they see a young person and they are simply afraid of them.

Young people regularly complained that adults, police, and other authority figures frequently hassled them. At a meeting of a Methodist youth group, two teenagers, James and Todd, discussed how police had stopped their friend Bill at a local restaurant on Friday night:

> JAMES: Straight! Bill was going in and there were cops at the gate. Bill was wearing his cap backwards and they pulled him in for being a gangbanger. They told him to take his cap off and took his name.
>
> TODD: What? For just wearing his cap backwards? That's stupid, they're stupid. It's if it's to the right or left—that's where it is if you're a gangbanger.
>
> JAMES: Yeah, but they were stopping everyone that looked like they could be in a gang. They were hassling me too and I'm not in a gang. Oh, but you should of seen it last night. There were Popes and Two Six [area gangs] everywhere. Man, it's going to be bad tonight!

Young people generally felt that they took all the blame for trouble in the neighborhood, as these comments by a thirteen-year-old member of the local Methodist youth group demonstrate:

> JENNY: Well, the cops have stopped me loads of times, saying that I was in a car with gangbangers and asking me who they were, just picking on us. I was in my brother's car and he got his window broken from some kids who are not from here. And then we were the ones that got into trouble. The cops

said that we must be in a gang and all that. We didn't shoot no one. It was kids from another neighborhood who did that.

Beltway adults often couched their views of youth in authoritarian terms. Michael Lufolli, a local police officer, explained how intergenerational relations work in his family: "Now in my house I am the boss. Whatever I say is right. I ask them to do one thing and that's to follow me blindly because I won't see them wrong. If I say it's dark outside they have to believe me because I'm telling them. If they do that then they won't get into trouble."

Residents occasionally talked about the need to reinstate physical punishment in schools, and the pervasive gang situation led some adults to consider extreme measures. For example, some BCL members advocated severe physical punishments for delinquents, such as the use of rubber hoses and other riot gear. These viewpoints did not reflect those of average residents, but they contributed to the strong emphasis on authoritarianism in Beltway. "I won't stand by and let this neighborhood go down the toilet," asserted one Beltwayite. "I'm not worried about these punks; I got these [*indicates his hands*] for my guns."

Young people in Beltway tended to respond to such views with alienation and hostility, turning a deaf ear and openly expressing their discontent. But while older Beltwayites evinced fear and distrust of young people, a sizable number of residents with young children were more willing to interact with youth in a positive way. For example, a number of residents volunteered their time and talents in after-school programs and math and science workshops, assisted in sports activities, helped with park maintenance, and lent a hand at summer day camp. Thus, a complex age stratification existed in Beltway.

ETHNIC CHANGE
AND THE FUTURE OF BELTWAY

For many years residents of Beltway had been concerned about the encroachment of people of color into their neighborhood, and they had confronted this challenge, as we have seen, with vigorous efforts to maintain a level of social organization that ensured neighborhood stability. In other words, using Hirschman's terminology (see Chapter One), the residents had developed a systematic pattern of voice to resist the penetration of people of color.[11] Over the years they had also displayed the kind of loyalty to the neighborhood that reinforces voice and counteracts or limits exit.

As has been noted, the relatively successful exercise of voice through neighborhood social organization over the years had been enhanced by several factors. These included a network of dense acquaintanceships, the presence of extended families, a high level of residential stability, vibrant community organizations, powerful local political ties, and common ethnic, racial, and class backgrounds.

However, the exercise of voice through neighborhood social organization also benefited from a common belief system, widely shared by the residents, that integrated social conservatism, patriotism, and sentiments concerning adherence to neighborhood standards. This belief system generated a clear set of specific behavioral norms: parents must supervise their children; residents are obligated to the community for the care and appearance of their property; and community members must stand together to resist graffiti, gangbangers, and other bad influences attributed to minorities and other outsiders. As has already been discussed, Beltwayites believed that if the neighborhood was allowed to deteriorate, some residents would be encouraged to leave. Blacks and Latinos from neighborhoods that border Beltway could then fill the vacancies.

Given Beltwayites' anxiety about keeping the neighborhood stable to prevent the penetration of minorities, the supervision of young people was a growing concern. Many Beltwayites, particularly the older residents, believed that young people posed a major threat to the social organization of the neighborhood. Accordingly, the hostility toward young people was palpable.

Nonetheless, despite the strenuous efforts of Beltway residents to keep their neighborhood stable and thereby control the influx of minorities, the latest census figures suggest that they are gradually losing the battle, and that residents themselves are cognizant that things are beginning to change—especially that the number and proportion of Latino homeowners is growing. As the principal of a local elementary and middle school put it, "I see more homes up for sale. But part of it is [whites leaving in response to perceived demographic changes in the neighborhood], and part of it is that there are older families. Moms and dads have stayed here, but the kids are not moving back here. They are selling homes."

We saw no evidence that real estate agents in Beltway were encouraging white flight: given the level of social organization in the neighborhood, launching and sustaining any kind of whispering campaign aimed at frightening homeowners would prove difficult. However, a gradual, but still limited, exit of white residents is clearly occurring. Of the response of residents to the changing face of the neighborhood, fifteen-year-old Tina Lupinski said, "They think that if one black family gets in, there goes the neighborhood. But the neighborhood has already been gone for a long time, but they don't even realize it." Nonetheless, the significant presence of municipal workers, who are required to live in the city, combined with Beltway's relatively strong level of social organization, might prevent the rapid mass exit of whites that Dover has experienced.

CHAPTER THREE

Dover

A Mixed Ethnic Community in Transition

————

Written with the collaboration of
Chenoa Flippen and Jolyon Wurr

Dover was first settled in the 1850s. The neighborhood struggled through economic decline and falling housing prices in the 1970s, stemming from industrial layoffs combined with an exodus of higher-income residents who bought homes in the suburbs. The property market revived in the 1980s, however, with an influx of Mexican Americans from neighboring communities.

Despite this influx, in 1990 almost two-thirds of Dover residents were white, including Eastern European immigrants as well as Americans of Irish, Italian, and German descent. However, Dover experienced an even more rapid change in population between 1990 and 2000. The Latino population almost tripled, while the white population dropped sharply, by more than half; Latinos constituted 77 percent of Dover's population in 2000, and whites only 19 percent (see Figure 3). The number of African American residents—although still very small—has also multiplied twelve-fold, while the small Asian and Pacific Islander population doubled.

FIGURE 3. DOVER: TOTAL POPULATIONS BY RACE AND HISPANIC ORIGIN, 1980–2000

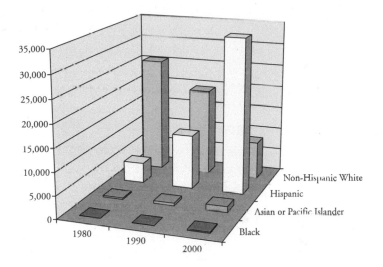

Longtime residents lamented this dramatic demographic shift, recalling that Dover was once a cohesive, close-knit, largely Polish community where everyone knew everyone else. Family networks were often dense, with people's grown siblings and children residing nearby, sometimes in the same multiunit building. One white woman in her late forties described the familiarity of her block while growing up in Dover:

> The three-story flat I grew up in was built by my grand-father. And my father's brother and his wife lived on the top floor, my two maiden aunts lived on the second floor, and my family lived in the garden apartment . . . And every house [on the block] was a three flat, and every house had two maiden aunts [*laughing*], one of whom was always named Stella. There was Mary and Stella on the corner—I don't remember the name of the two aunts—and then next door there was another Stella, and then my aunt and Stella lived upstairs . . . [My mother] rented it out for a long time to a friend—a widowed friend, the second floor, after my aunt died.

Dover also featured a well-developed shopping thorough-fare and other small stores scattered throughout the neighborhood, including grocery stores, ethnic specialty shops, clothing chains, restaurants, beauty salons and barbershops, bars and taverns, a movie theater, and a variety of professional services. These venues provided additional opportunities for social interaction. A former Dover resident spoke of the importance of chance encounters in the shopping district:

> It's interesting, but when I was growing up, there was not much interaction among the women. They stayed in their houses, they took care of the children, and occasionally on summer nights people would get to-

gether. But there were no coffee get-togethers; people did not do a lot of visiting . . . They worked. They cleaned. They cleaned all day. They would chat when they were doing marketing—I mean, when they were doing shopping. When they were doing their grocery shopping they would meet—I mean, it was terrible to be a child, because then your mother would just stop and talk, and talk, and talk, and talk . . . But that was the real socializing they did. And I've thought about that, a number of years ago. And I thought, if you talk when you meet someone on the street, when you're shopping, then you're still working. It's not as if you sat down with someone and purposely said you were going to have a good time in the middle of the day . . . [Because] you can't say, "I baked a cake, would you come to my house?" Because then you'd just be— what?—sitting and drinking coffee. With all that work to do.

Several large factories employed many neighborhood residents, further fostering community ties and unity.[1] Those who grew up in the area said that adults monitored and disciplined the children in the neighborhood, and these long-time residents attributed their respect for authority to this accountability.

Rapid population turnover, along with the growth of large shopping malls and the relocation of factories away from Dover, disrupted these bonds of association, built up over decades. School activist David Sidone attested:

Yeah . . . All of that is changing with society. You know, I remember a time when I was a kid—God forbid I did something wrong on the block next to mine, my mother knew it within five minutes. Chances are, if it was someone we knew long enough, she'd grab hold of me and rap me upside my head. You know? You don't have that no more because unfortunately today in this society it's all, "I'll sue you . . . if you touch my kid."

While doing laundry, our field researchers overheard a conversation between two white women apparently in their late forties. The first woman greeted the second and then said, "Hey, Delores, are you still bowling?" Delores replied, "No, all my wives are gone. They all moved." They then talked at length about how difficult it was to find things to do now that so many of their old friends no longer lived in the area.

Language and cultural differences between white and Latino residents also curbed prospects for close friendships and block-level unity. The 1990 census revealed that nearly 15 percent of the population struggled with basic English-language skills, and by 2000 that figure had ballooned to 42 percent.[2]

A young Latino working at a local real estate office who had moved from Mexico to Chicago five years earlier—first to a well-established Latino enclave, then to Dover—expressed his frustration with his inability to communicate with his neighbors. While holding down two jobs, he had not found time to learn English, and although he reported that his neighbors often worked in their yards, he felt he could not even greet them.

Age differences often exacerbated ethnic differences. As established white residents aged, their involvement in the community and with their neighbors decreased. Children fostered social contact, as residents with youngsters often spent time with the parents of their children's friends, car-pooling, exchanging babysitters, sharing school and religious activities, and addressing school concerns. Drawing on her forty-one years as a homeowner in Dover, an elderly white woman walking home with groceries from a supermarket around the corner described her relationships with her neighbors as good but not as strong as they once were. When her children were small, she said, she regularly talked over the fence with neighbors while they watched their children playing in the yard. Whereas she once socialized with everyone on her block, at the time of the interview she knew only four or five families, and she observed that people now tend to keep to themselves, as fewer lifelong residents remained in Dover.

NEIGHBORHOOD DEMOGRAPHIC CHANGE AND ETHNIC ANTAGONISMS

Despite the significant ethnic turnover, some Dover residents expressed positive attitudes toward neighbors of different ethnicities. For example, the white principal of a local elementary school remarked, "It's an interesting neighborhood because we have a lot of different people—people from different ethnic groups . . . And I think that's what makes this community so unique. We have all kinds of people: Polish, Spanish, black, Italian. Everything!" Many Latino store owners reported positive experiences with white owners of neighboring businesses, and Latinos and whites often encountered one another in the workplace, especially in local restaurants, where they developed close personal relationships. White resident Jerry Budinski commented:

> I mean, the prices for homes in the area are attractive. They're high. A lot of people want to move into here. You know the area has had an influx of Hispanics . . . We don't view that as a negative. Those people— I mean we have a nice neighborhood. Those people saw it as a nice neighborhood. And they want to come here and keep it as a nice neighborhood, you know. They . . . don't look like they are here to trash the place. They look like they are here because they want to be part of it. And they play a role in opening businesses on [Main Street]. So they are not only a part of the residential community, but they're part of the business community too. So it's a credit to the whole area.

At a meeting of the Knights of Lithuania, a local church group, an older white woman commented, "There's a lot of newcomers now. The Mexicans, they're good to have. They come in and fix up their places. They put on new siding and things like that. A lot of them are builders, and they do the work themselves." Another older white woman, standing in front of her one-story brick bungalow, stated that Dover is a good neighborhood with "lots of green grass and flowers" and "ethnic roots." She added as an afterthought, "You know, I don't mind them coming in, as long as they keep their property up."

However, while some white residents viewed their Latino neighbors as decent, industrious people, many others regarded Latinos as lawless and dirty. In a city renowned for the ethnic character of its neighborhoods, many white residents felt that Mexicans had stolen Dover's identity; as a result, they moved to Beltway and other mostly white neighborhoods in the Chicago metropolitan area. For residents who were more tolerant of a Latino presence, social networks were generally limited to second-generation Mexican Americans who had better English-language skills.

When asked whether Dover was a nice neighborhood, most white people responded that it was very much in decline and openly expressed resentment toward their Latino neighbors, blaming them for defacing public property and reducing public safety. Patronela, a woman of Polish descent who had lived in the neighborhood for thirty-two years, reported, "They're a different nationality—strange people. They come and go. They don't care about the neighborhood." An older Lithuanian man on the street had lived in the neighborhood for more than two decades and worked in a local bar. He had recently moved to the suburbs, but he returned to visit his son, who still lived in the community:

> It's going down—the whole neighborhood. The Mexicans are coming in, and they don't care. It's different

now. They don't care. They just start moving in and they want your neighborhood. They don't want you in it, they want it. Now it is all just Mexicans. They put up graffiti, mark up the garage doors . . .

A white woman who grew up in Dover revealed that her animosity toward Latinos had grown as their numbers had increased:

When I was growing up it was much more homogenous . . . And we had, I remember, a good percentage of Mexican children [who] went to school with us. I was just telling him [*pointing to her son*] about this, in fact. And there didn't seem to be any prejudice at the time. So that's changing as the neighborhood changes to largely Hispanic.

When asked whether there was more prejudice in Dover now than when Latinos initially arrived, she responded, "Yes, there is. Well, I mean, the people who have remained [here] are largely my parents' age. My mother will be seventy-five next year. And the crime has gone up in the neighborhood, which frightens older people."

Several white residents expressed contradictory views. Konrad, for example, commented on how hard Mexican immigrants worked, saying that many local businesses would "go under" if immigrants were not willing to hold low-skill, low-paying jobs. Yet moments later he maintained that Mexicans were "riffraff" who were responsible for rising crime rates.

Tensions between whites and Latinos clearly bubbled just below the surface, occasionally erupting in public settings over the issue of language: English versus Spanish. Many Latino residents felt as though language barriers excluded them from community life, while some Eastern European immigrants and their descendants felt that the Mexicans were not trying to learn English. An exchange at one public meeting illustrated the wall of resistance longtime residents had constructed against Latino efforts to include Spanish alongside English in the town's civic and commercial activities. A Latino man in his thirties stood before the microphone in a room filled with at least a hundred Dover residents and a handful of local politicians and chastised organizers for not providing material in Spanish. Although an interpreter was translating the proceedings, a community calendar appeared only in English.

The man's criticism provoked a wave of audible disagreement from the crowd, and a white woman yelled from the back of the crowded room, "This is America!" The man then reiterated his contention that the community should do more to accomodate Spanish-speaking residents who had not yet learned English, an opinion echoed by a Latina seated in the front row. Signs of commotion swept through the audience, and the white woman fired back, "Well, what about the Poles, then?"—referring to the many Polish residents who, in their recollection, had made the painful transition from their native tongue to English without the help requested by the Latino community.[3]

Some white residents considered calls by Latinos to provide public information in Spanish to be arrogant and an affront to the American way of life. People sorted themselves by ethnicity at most gatherings, including park festivals and sidewalk sales. For instance, one disgruntled white father and his family left a free play at a festival in a local park when the actors onstage began switching between English and Spanish.

The daily struggle over territory and pride ranged from the strategic placement of U.S. and Mexican flags to neighbors' taste in music. At a summer festival sponsored by a local church, someone teased a white woman about the polka music playing over the loudspeaker. She replied, "Yeah, I kinda like it, though. Over where my husband and I live, the air is always full of that Mexican music. Me and my husband, we put our speakers out on the back porch and just blast it. It's like music wars over there."

Mexican residents, unwilling to dilute their cultural practices, also expressed resentment toward their white neighbors. Victor, a young Latino who had just recently moved from a Latino enclave to the east, replied, "It's really quiet . . . when I leave Pilsen and go [to Dover], it's amazing. Everybody keeps to themselves. *No Saludan!* [They don't say hello!] My neighbor is really grouchy. I say 'hi' to him and he just ignores me. But I think it's because our skin is a few shades too dark." When asked if the neighbor was Mexican, Victor replied, "No! I think he's Polish or something. But there's a lot of Mexicans moving in there. It's really changing fast."

In Dover, recent Mexican arrivals were generally younger than the more established white residents, and this led many whites to link the presence of Latinos with crime, especially gang-related crime imported from nearby neighborhoods. According to one resident, "The problems come in with the Americanized Mexican kids. These kids have no morals or values." Olimpia, the white director of a Dover institution for the handicapped, described the change in Dover since her arrival in the 1960s:

> When I first came here it was a very ethnic neighborhood, and it was a very Polish, Lithuanian, European-type area, and everybody took great pride in the appearance of their homes, and their lawns, and everybody had little gardens in the backs, and the alleys were beautiful and everything was so clean . . . It was totally white, European. And now it has totally changed. Now there's graffiti on different stores. We have problems with strange people hanging around in the alleys, people who are intoxicated. We have problems now with the liquor store, street people coming around, more people ringing our doorbell wanting food, wanting money. Our cars have been vandalized; some cars have been stolen from the parking lot . . . That kind of change. It has drastically changed. Now very much a mixture, there are Chinese, Mexicans, Afro-Americans, the whole mixture. There are Indians . . . all kinds of different cultures. And many more teenagers.

As the most tangible symbol of gang presence, graffiti was a constant concern. Lawrence, a longtime local business owner and civic leader, captured the anxiety over declining community safety when he said:

> [Dover] used to be nice, but, no offense to anyone, these people are coming in and things are changing. They're putting their graffiti everywhere. They're not keeping up the property. The other residents try very hard to keep the neighborhood clean, but they get real disheartened about the cleaning. It's not like it was in my parents' day, when people could sleep on the side-walk when it was hot, in the summer. People really did, they pulled the mattresses right off the beds and slept outside. No one worried about it. My mother used to go downtown all the time and never locked the door . . . Now, well, you can't even think of doing that!

A white female bartender commented on the graffiti:

> Oh, it breaks my heart. It makes me so mad what they did to that building. It never used to be like that . . . You want to know why they do that to the buildings? It's their way of saying they want whitey out of the neighborhood . . . You know, these [Latino] kids, you walk down the street—they won't even move over for you. You have to walk around. It never used to be like that.

Graffiti adorning the wall in the men's washroom at a local doughnut shop and diner included invectives such as

FUCK ALL SPICS and KILL ALL GANGBANGERS. Joan, a white woman who grew up in the community, pointed to the importance of generational factors in the tensions between white and Latino residents of Dover:

FIELD-WORKER: So what did most people think when more and more Mexicans started moving into the neighborhood? How did people react to that?

JOAN: I think they were—I think the Polish felt—the Polish people were frightened. I still think they are. I think a lot of people moved because they were frightened. Well, [my friend's] mother and father were robbed by two young Mexicans, who burglarized their house . . . But see, I think that happens in neighborhoods that age, and the population that preys on them does not have to be a different ethnic group.

FIELD-WORKER: So you mean they're more interested in generational than ethnic?

JOAN: I think that it happens, but of course people are going to say, "It's because the Mexicans are here, that this is happening."

FIELD-WORKER: And of course crime rates are going up all over the city, too, so . . .

JOAN: Right.

FIELD-WORKER: But you think people perceive that it has to do with the Mexicans?

JOAN: They do . . . That's what people say, that . . . it's because they're Mexican or because they're black.

But there's things that are happening in the
neighborhood as the population ages, as the
housing stock ages, that would be happening if you
had any influx of younger, poorer people. That's
exactly what's happening . . . I know that people
perceive that it's because people are black, or
Mexican. But that's not what's happening.

White residents reported that they no longer let their
children play outside without adult supervision, and community leaders commented that residents were less likely to
intervene with local wayward youth out of fear of retaliation.
Concerns ranged from slashed tires to spray-painted garage
doors to physical assaults and gunshots. According to Father
Tom, a local priest:

It's quite different from the neighborhood in which I
grew up . . . where they knew everyone, and they knew
the minute somebody different came into the neighborhood. And it's not just [Dover]. It's everywhere . . .
There's always fear of retaliation, you know. So you
have to be careful about if I'm going to yell, will I get
my windows broken, or something like that. This is,
you know, this is quite different from what existed
before. If I had been out of line as a ten-year-old, my
mother would have heard about it from a neighbor.

Said William Nadroski, a local business owner and longtime Dover resident who with his wife and children moved

out of the community because they felt it was too dangerous: "Years ago, when I was growing up around here, kids fought with their fists. Now they carry guns and knives—mostly guns. Life means nothing to them—they'd shoot you in a second."

Such fear of Latino youth prompted many senior white residents to rely on the police rather than face-to-face relations to redress even minimal disturbances. One white man who had lived in the neighborhood for more than twenty years said that his friends routinely called the police to have their Mexican neighbors' cars towed whenever they blocked the alley rather than risking confrontation. And a principal at a local elementary school commented, "I know definitely the white people constantly are calling the police . . . They don't want graffiti."

One young Latino male who had recently moved to Dover complained that his white neighbors had called the police to protest noise from a small backyard party. According to Luis, a car full of white police officers arrived and demanded that the party disperse. The host of the party barely spoke English and did not understand why he could not drink beer and listen to music in his own backyard: "So the next thing, the cop calls for backup, and two more squads come. It was like six cops out there . . . So finally, they were forced inside . . . All because of Archie Bunker— you know I call him that because he's like the stereotype of an old white guy who hates all immigrants. But this is what it's like!"

Ethnicity exacerbated common tensions between young

and old regarding spending on schools and other services for children, such as daycare.[4] In 1990, although the community at large was roughly 37 percent Latino, all the local schools except for one magnet school were more than 60 percent Latino, and Dover Latinos expressed great concern about the quality of public education, while the older white population focused on benefits and services for seniors. This cleavage encouraged competition for scarce public funds and further strained social networks.

Ethnic tensions among neighbors undermined block-level social interaction and inhibited the formation of social networks. Residents who perceived neighborhood decline also distanced themselves from community affairs. The retreat of white residents averse to the growing Mexican presence hastened the breakdown of social networks, as many of those who had chosen to stay, or who could not afford to move, appeared to have withdrawn from community life.

Forty years ago, Dover residents united in overlapping organizations, as business owners, homemakers, school officials, and politicians attended the same churches and served on the same boards, and their children went to school together. However, Dover's rapid neighborhood transition posed a serious challenge to such social groups and networks. In the face of neighborhood transition, organizations in Dover had declined, divided along ethnic lines, or united internally through inter-ethnic networks and coalitions.[5]

BUSINESS AND CIVIC ORGANIZATIONS
IN DECLINE

Faced with a growing Latino population, white members of local business and civic associations could attempt to include new Latino members, exclude them, or do nothing. These associations generally followed the third path: inaction appears to have prevailed because of a lack of network ties that would have been effective in reaching and recruiting Latino members. The result is that existing groups have shrunk as their members have aged, and no new members have replaced them.

Similarly, incoming Latino residents could seek to join existing business organizations, start new ones, or remain uninvolved. Again, Dover Latinos largely followed the third course. Young Mexicans composed the majority of new entrants to Dover, and they remained largely outside of organizational networks. Civic organizations tended to attract people with leisure time, and long working hours often kept the substantial proportion of Latino residents who were recent immigrants or low-wage earners from becoming socially involved. Participation in civic associations also correlated strongly with education, and many Latino residents of Dover had strikingly low levels of education.[6]

The past—often recalled in a glorified manner—left longtime residents dissatisfied with the current state of affairs in Dover. Educational activist David Sidone noted, "There's no boys' club in the area, there's no YMCA in the area, there's no organizations in the area."

The Dover Community Conservation Council (DCCC)—which once counted several prominent community leaders among its membership but had recently attracted very few newcomers—offered an example of organizational decline. Most long-term residents of Dover remembered the DCCC's annual home and garden contests. While these events were designed to foster community connections and often drew members from several organizational spheres, by the early 1990s many longtime participants had died or moved away and the DCCC had all but ceased to function. According to DCCC president Raymond Tims:

> The Conservation Council isn't that active anymore . . . See, many of the members are getting old, or have died, and the community's changing . . . Our purposes and goals have diminished. The garden contest, that was to award people who kept up nice gardens, and so forth. Now we give that money for the scholarships. The community is changing, and there are a lot of new people, and we don't know what they're thinking.

Jon Christjanson, the Dover Business Association (DBA) president, who also edited the neighborhood newspaper, concurred with Tims's assessment of the DCCC:

> They used to have a big festival. I don't know how active they are now. The problem with that is that a lot of their members, their organizing members, were—

are—older people. They're seniors. And, you know, they pass away or become no longer able to participate, and there are no younger people really coming in. They would sponsor these garden contests and they'd give an award for the best-looking garden, the most improvements, and the best-looking house. And they'd have all these different categories, you know; apartments and two flats and single homes. The culmination was this big festival at the firehouse . . . And they would have photographers there to take pictures of the prizewinners, and the alderman would come and give them their awards and certificates. They'd have a band come and play—the band from [a local high school]—and sometimes priests would come.

The DBA offered another example of organizational decline in Dover. In the first half of the 1980s, the DBA successfully applied for city development funds and used them to sponsor community events and business promotions. However, after years of accelerated residential and business turnover and cutbacks in development funding by city government, the DBA was barely functioning. Jon Christjanson recognized this:

At one time [the DBA] was quite active and quite strong. Right now it's not as active as it once was. Originally the group qualified for the community development block grants . . . provided by the city. So we were able to do more promotions. You know, we used to have turkey giveaways and contests with prizes and events for the other holidays. The budget cuts have made these things a lot harder. [Municipal authorities have] cut back all over the city. We've had to pare down our activities accordingly and have the organization be more self-sufficient.

Without exception, residents who mentioned the DCCC and the DBA felt that those groups were no longer as active as they had once been. "They're both in kind of a transitional phase," maintained Dan Lampert, a community leader. "They're having problems . . . They're more subdued now."

Similarly, the local branch of the Kiwanis Club, a fraternal civic organization, was active in the community for decades and once provided a number of services, but now it, too, suffered from dwindling membership and funds. A white man who worked for twenty-seven years as a teacher, assistant principal, and principal at a local elementary school had this to say:

I think that [Dover] is a community in transition right now. I think that the organizations that may have existed in the past are bowing out to a certain extent. The [Dover branch of the] Kiwanis comes to mind. They've been a very good organization previously . . . Well, I don't know if they're bowing out, but what I'm saying is there's a change in people. People who may have been active in the community for a long time perhaps are not here any longer. And new organizations haven't had an opportunity to take root.

At a monthly board meeting, the few active Kiwanians complained about the club's lack of support from local business and political leaders. The national organization stipulates that each chapter maintain a minimum number of members to retain its charter, and Dover's Kiwanis Club had been well below that minimum for years. The number of attendees at regular lunch meetings fell so low that the restaurant that had hosted them for nearly a decade no longer wanted to reserve the small back room for the group, and two annual fundraisers no longer generated the capital they once did.

The Kiwanis charter also stipulates that no more than two members of each local chapter can hold the same occupation, but years ago the group made exceptions for educators, in order to remain solvent. Thus the Dover Kiwanis had increasingly become an organization of teachers, and each school felt compelled to have a representative so it would not be forgotten when the club distributed its funds, as schools were the main beneficiaries.

Even bending the rules, the organization faced extreme difficulty in meeting its membership minimum. The situation became so severe that the group called a special meeting and decided to send members a warning that the chapter was in danger of closing if membership did not grow. This letter informed members that they were required to attend a conference, and each member was to bring two potential new members. Yet only a handful of registered members showed up at the "mandatory" meeting, and they brought only three new people, none of whom pledged to join that night. Attendees explicitly discussed the fact that the neighborhood was "changing," and acknowledged the need to reach out to Mexican newcomers to survive, but they did not know how to do so. Of twenty-eight registered Kiwanians, most of whom had fallen into lapsed status, only two were Latino, and members did not recruit any new Latino members for a second "do-or-die" meeting.

A speech by Kiwanis president Sam Goddard, an assistant principal of the local high school who grew up in the community, included his reflection on the critical gap between the group's desire to reach out to the Latino community and actual steps being taken toward that end:

> We need to go to the businesses. Maybe not the small businesses, because let's face it, the neighborhood's changing. But we could. That's an option. We could go to all those small businesses, those restaurants, and ask them if they want to join. But we still have corporations. We still have Dover Bank.

No one followed up on his reference to small Mexican businesses. Rather than testing innovative strategies to lure younger Latino members, these traditional residents instead fell back on their old networks and sent letters to the few large businesses in the area. Participants ended the meeting by solemnly declaring, "If we don't get new members, let's lay the club to rest."

THE CATHOLIC CHURCH
AND ETHNIC DIVISION

Mexicans tend to be highly religious and retain ties to their Roman Catholic faith, and priests and other church officials, both in Dover and citywide, had traditionally encouraged that participation. There are more than a dozen Catholic churches within Dover's boundaries, and parishes have long been important institutions in the area. However, despite their common faith, Mexicans and Poles did not come together in churches. In fact, local churches exemplified the second of three possible responses to neighborhood change: they had divided along ethnic lines, and what appeared to be an ideal venue for integration had instead trended toward segregation. Several Dover churches catered mainly to either Poles or Lithuanians, while mixed parishes suffered from bitter internal divisions.

Many white church members—alienated by Spanish-language services for a growing number of Latinos—attended only English-language Masses or neighborhood churches where English was still the norm. Two of the most established churches—including the parish that sponsored Pope John Paul II's historic visit to Chicago in 1979—continued to serve Eastern European ethnic groups almost exclusively. This church held Masses in Polish and English and printed church newsletters and announcements in both languages. While the parish priest acknowledged that more Latinos were arriving in the community, the church made no effort to offer church services in Spanish.

Another church provided a good example of a parish that had divided internally along ethnic lines. The church's congregation was initially split between two churches—St. Francis and Sacred Heart. As part of a diocese-wide closing of congregations with declining membership, leaders reassigned members of St. Francis to Sacred Heart, and the priest at St. Francis followed his flock to the new location. While both churches had strong Polish traditions, St. Francis was predominantly Mexican by the time the churches merged. The archdiocese decided to rename the newly consolidated parish, and the mostly Polish parishioners from Sacred Heart wanted to call it St. Anne. The merged church instead became Our Lady of Mary, in veneration of the patroness of the Americas.

The white parishioners resented this name change, and also felt that the priest from St. Francis favored his Mexican parishioners in assigning people to positions of authority. While Sacred Heart had not offered Spanish-language Masses, St. Francis had done so for more than ten years; when the two churches merged, many white parishioners resented this addition to the worship. These members felt that Mexicans had "taken over" the church, and even whites not connected to the church agreed.

Father Davis, the pastor at Our Lady of Mary, while acknowledging rancor and competition between white and Latino churchgoers, pointed out that rivalries had existed between non-Latino white ethnic groups long before Spanish-speaking Catholics arrived:

And that doesn't persist now, except now we've got a new rivalry. And maybe even "rivalry" is a polite word. Now we've got a real dislike between the Spanish and the whites. And there's a lot of complaining on the part of the old-timers that we're catering too much to the Mexicans by offering the Spanish services that we offer. They feel they should learn English like we had to do, like our parents had to do, when we, when they immigrated here.

A third-generation Polish American whose parents had been very active at Sacred Heart similarly noted that "the people's feelings are still very bitter and still very high, and most of the bitterness is from the people who—like my parents— held positions in the parish and had been active. And it's not just a power thing as much as giving your time and your money, and all of a sudden finding yourself like a second-class citizen."

Father Davis elaborated on the origin of the divisions within the parish:

I don't think it's just the difference in language. Maybe—I mean, that might be a little part of it. I think it's just a form of racism. That was true when these all white churches were gradually turning black [in other neighborhoods]. There, with African American people moving in, they did not share the same faith. They all went to Baptist churches for the most part. Very few of them came to the Catholic Church, but those that did, they spoke the same language but because of the different race there was, you know, tremendous antagonism on the part of the whites especially. And that's the way it is here; I notice the whites are more antagonistic than the Hispanics are . . . [They say,] "We are the ones that built these places and now look who's coming and taking them over and they're not giving."

As a result of such tension, the church conducted Masses in Spanish in the morning and in English in the afternoon, so ethnic groups had little opportunity to interact. (Other churches alternated Polish and English Masses throughout the day.) A negligible number of Latinos attended English services, and virtually no whites participated in the Spanish services. Not surprisingly, church groups divided along similar lines. One woman among a group of older white church members setting up booths for a summer festival indignantly scoffed at the "Hispanic booth" and asked, "What do they need their own booth for?" Several other Dover residents made passing comments about ethnic divisions within the churches. No one expressed the view that the Catholic Church might have helped Latinos assimilate into the community.

SCHOOLS AND ETHNIC UNITY

Schools in Dover illustrate the third possible pattern of response to ethnic change: integration and unification. All schools in the neighborhood maintained bilingual committees and staff members who could speak both English and Spanish, and school representatives in Dover did not mention ethnic conflict.[7] The schools also devoted great attention to Mexican culture and sponsored events for Cinco de Mayo and other fiesta days.

One Dover elementary school, for example, made visible efforts to accommodate its sizable Mexican student population, as the plethora of Spanish-speaking employees and Latino decorations lining the hallways attested. A bilingual committee addressed language issues and sponsored Mexican cultural events throughout the school year. The school even funded a full-time community representative to help Latino parents tap into educational opportunities and local programs. The white school principal expressed sympathy for the problems of immigrants and solicited Latino volunteers from the local electric company to act as mentors for her students. And unlike some in the community who resented residents who spoke only Spanish, the principal faulted herself for not being fluent in Spanish, and insisted on offering real-time Spanish translation at local school council meetings even if few Latino parents were present.

Bilingual Latinas actively supported parents with poor English skills and helped them gain access to information. At one school, the white principal commented that one mother, a Mexican immigrant on the school's LSC, served as a liaison for scores of Latina parents. This woman lunched with other Latina mothers every Monday to discuss issues that affected their children, creating an important informal network and helping to solidify access to school channels. According to the principal, this woman not only enabled parents without English proficiency to express their concerns but was also able to provide the principal with a valuable perspective on the concerns of a sizable portion of his students.

Several community leaders commented on the high degree of cooperation in the schools. Asked if he felt the community was cohesive, for example, the priest at the predominantly Polish Catholic church replied:

> It used to be. I don't think it's as cohesive anymore. And I think it will take some time . . . to have Anglos, Hispanics, and new immigrant Poles work together harmoniously . . . There're beginnings of this. We're doing it in the [public] school. I think it's the only place that I see that done . . . [Otherwise] it's living side by side but not touching.

Why did whites respond favorably to Latino participation in the schools, and why did Latinos respond constructively to white efforts to foster inclusion, in sharp contrast to other community settings, such as churches? Neighborhood schools had become severely overcrowded owing to the sharp increase in Dover's Latino population since 1980, even as the community's white population was shrinking. Overenrollment plagued not only Dover elementary schools but also threatened Dover High School, as each successive cohort of students grew larger. (In 1992, for example, the high school enrolled 186 seniors, 302 juniors, 474 sophomores, and 775 freshmen.)[8] Faced with the prospect of busing their children to neighboring poor black schools, whites and Latinos with school-age children put aside their differences and created powerful networks among Latino and white parents, and among parents and school and city officials—albeit heavily colored with anti-black sentiment.

The Chicago Board of Education originally responded to overcrowding by allocating millions of dollars for new schools. However, apparently due to site-selection problems, most of the proposed schools had not been built by the mid-1990s. The Board of Education therefore ordered that Dover children be bused to "underutilized" schools in Stockton, a nearby African American neighborhood. While Dover schools were overwhelmingly white and Latino—three of the five elementary schools had less than 1 percent African American students—the elementary school that received most of the Dover children, Chaney, was over 80 percent African American and under 1 percent non-Latino white.

White and Latino parents came together in great numbers to oppose busing and to stress the need for new schools, expressing a strong preference for even portable classrooms over busing. The fact that the underutilized schools were predominantly black was significant. Many busing opponents argued that the receiver schools were inferior and located in dangerous neighborhoods, and statements about the safety and quality of education nearly always reflected attitudes about race.

The neighborhood to which the Dover students were to be bused was one of many Chicago neighborhoods that saw rapid racial turnover in the 1950s, as the black population exploded from 0.4 percent in 1940 to 13 percent in 1950 and over 90 percent in 1960. By 1990 the neighborhood also housed more than four times as many families with incomes below the poverty line than did Dover, and further recorded 37 percent more juvenile contacts with the police and 60 percent more court referrals of juvenile offenders than did Dover in 1980.

Participants in LSC meetings, where whites and Latinos worked well together, repeatedly raised the safety issue. At one meeting, a white principal announced that schools that could make room for more students were either "west of Pullman [Avenue] or north of Constitution [Avenue], so any parents that want to send their kids have to send them that way." He said he did not forward any busing applications to parents because of "where the schools [with openings] are," adding that they were a long distance away. Miguel, who worked at the local bus terminal as a mechanic and was active in both the LSC and a district-wide overcrowding commit-tee, commented that the proposed schools were in a "mostly black area." The principal concurred and further noted, "You can have a totally safe school that the kids are going to, but there's no guarantee that the kids are safe going there. There's nobody who can guarantee the safety of the kids while they're going through those neighborhoods."

Speakers at the LSC meeting repeatedly referred to the fact that parents would keep their children home rather than send them to "dangerous" schools outside Dover as part of their efforts to encourage administrators and parents to oppose overcrowding but resist busing. At one public meeting, Dan Lampert, cofounder of the Dover–McAdam Park Cluster—a grassroots group established in 1991 in response to frustration over the failed promises of state, city, and school bureaucracies—expressed his strong views: "We have kids out there not going to school! We've got parents not letting their kids be bused into bad neighborhoods, so the kids just aren't going, and I'm one of them parents! What are we going to do, ladies and gentlemen?"

In interviews, several other residents, including principals and LSC members, made similar statements. Mrs. Fuentes, a Latina representative of the Dover school district, sympathetically explained the parents' perspective:

[Latinos] work real hard and save their money so they can move into a nice house right across the street from a good school, and they don't know why they can't send their kids there. It's very hard. They end up having to send their kids to school in a neighborhood that's even worse than the one they just came from. I can't tell them what to do. I can't tell them they have to send their kids there. I tell them that it's against the law [to keep their kids home], but I can't tell them not to do it.

Indirectly reinforcing the link between race and opposition to busing, one principal referred to the lack of resistance to busing Dover children to nonblack communities:

We respond to the parents, and what—basically, it's what we get in yelling, it is what we get in tears: that they can't get their kid into a school. And I'm the controlled enrollment school and my kids are being bused out. And I get usually with those parents that are crying. And then they tell me that they won't send their child to school—anywhere. And in many instances, they don't . . . The prime school that they get bused to is an underutilized school . . . Just recently, a couple months ago, we were able to have kids bused to Pilsen. That's far more acceptable to the parents.

When asked why Pilsen was preferable to Chaney, the principal replied, "Pilsen is a Hispanic neighborhood. [Chaney] is predominantly—is a black school. But it's particularly—the parents aren't opposed to, you know, its being black. They're opposed to the area it's located in. It's not really what mothers consider a safe neighborhood."

Some busing opponents asserted that busing was costly and would undermine neighborhood cohesion. The Latino husband of the white LSC chairwoman at Ellison Elementary made the latter objection at a district-wide meeting on overcrowding: "When we went to school, we knew everyone there. We knew our friends' parents, and they knew us. It was a real community. We're robbing our kids of that. We're splitting up the community."

A representative from a school outside Dover that was also suffering from severe overcrowding countered, "Maybe that's exactly what we need. By not splitting communities you'll end up with Latinos in [Archer Park], whites in [Dover], blacks in [Stockton]. We'll just be reinforcing the image of Chicago as the most highly segregated city in the country. Parents come and don't want their kids to go to school in black areas. We need to get over that hurdle, that's all." The Latino responded, "That's very idealistic, but this is reality we're dealing with. Not ideals, reality." His wife, the LSC chairwoman, added, "There's a lot of fear out there."

White and Latino participants in the first district-wide meeting of the newly elected overcrowding committee in 1994—headed by Sarah Lampert, Cluster cofounder— repeatedly talked about race, and the meeting sometimes became quite tense. After listening to roughly an hour of complaints about the Board of Education's broken promises to build new schools, a Latina district official said, "We're just going to have to come to terms with an unhappy solution. There is a solution here, and it's to bus these kids to underutilized schools where the students are black, in neighborhoods that are black."

This comment met with immediate disapproval from the audience, whose members countered with protests about the inferior quality of education at underutilized schools. Unperturbed, the district official maintained that several of the schools in question were excellent, both well funded and well staffed, and pointed out that they included a magnet school, but these schools remained undersubscribed because parents did not want to send their children to schools that serve a predominantly black population. A woman affiliated with the magnet school interjected, "The hardest thing to do is convince people it's not so bad going to a black school." A Latino replied:

> It's not that they're afraid of black schools. There's nothing wrong with black schools. It's just that, well, we watch the news. You see it every day. Blacks are scared of their own neighborhoods! You read in the paper all the time about blacks moving back South to get away from the crime and the drugs. There's no quality there [in the black neighborhood]. We need to get some property here in the city. When business needs something, they get it, right? Why doesn't that happen with the Board of Education? Why can't we get something for our kids?

The presence of a K-8 magnet school in Dover aggravated the situation. Established in the early 1980s under a consent decree between the Chicago school district and the federal government, magnet schools must enroll equal numbers of black, white, and Latino students. In Dover, the magnet program set up shop in a large and handsome building at the center of the neighborhood. While the school had seen isolated incidents of racial violence, its magnet status did not originally provoke organized opposition. However, when the city began to bus Dover children out of the community, parents began clamoring that the school be "turned over" to the neighborhood. Even though three hundred of the seven hundred children attending the magnet school already resided in Dover, parents of children who had not gained admission argued that neighborhood residents should receive priority.

Anti-busing activists repeatedly referred to the number of buses that arrived at the magnet school from outside the community. At one LSC meeting, for example, Sarah Lampert yelled out indignantly, "Seventeen buses a day come into the magnet school, and our kids are being shipped out!" The outcry over the magnet school had garnered political attention. At another LSC meeting, State Representative Joseph Ruiz said:

> I have a bill this session that's going to require magnet schools like [this one] to admit students from within the community first. And then, if there's room, kids from outside the school. There's seventeen bus loads of children from outside this community coming in. Two blocks away, you have classrooms that average between forty-eight and fifty-two. That's crazy. How do you tell a parent that, no, your child cannot go to the school that's right across the street from the home you just bought? In fact, we're going to put them on a bus and ship them over to [a predominantly African American neighborhood].

The fact that the magnet school was operating below capacity was a point of contention. Dan Lampert's impassioned remarks at a special LSC meeting called to address overcrowding at Ellison Elementary were typical:

We want additions immediately! All the schools in this entire area are overcrowded except one. The magnet school is at 60 percent capacity. There are people out there not even sending their kids to school so their kids won't have to get bused. And if you ask me, that's not right. You will put me in jail first before I bus my kids out of my community!

The audience of mostly Latina mothers and their small children greeted Lampert's comments with rousing applause. Encouraged, he continued:

We've been addressing this problem for twenty years! . . . We're sick and tired of servicing other communities while our own community is not getting serviced! We're tired of the rhetoric, tired of the lies, tired of the manipulations from City Hall, the Board of Education, and the bureaucrats.

The magnet school enrolled by far the most African Americans of any school in the neighborhood: 25 percent. Of six other elementary schools, only one enrolled more than 5 percent black students. When asked if opposition to busing was based on race, the magnet school's white male principal answered:

I would think that you would probably find people of varying opinions. One of the principals in the area wrote a letter, which I still have a copy of, which simply said that one of the solutions to the overcrowding in the Dover area would be to get rid of, I'm trying to quote it, "Get rid of the nonresident children in the community." And the nonresidential children in the community are African American.

Whether safety, educational quality, racism, or a combination of all three had spurred the fight against busing, one middle-aged Latino school official emphasized that overcrowding alone was not enough to encourage parents to act:

These parents are happy if their kids can go to school here. If their kids get into a community school, they're satisfied, and don't feel the need to get involved. They don't realize that they're getting screwed and their kids are getting screwed. They don't realize the full impact of having forty or more kids in a classroom. They're just happy their kids are in, and they settle for all this bullshit from the Board [of Education].

The Cluster—one of the only organizations in Dover that continued to attract new members—reflected considerable Latino-white integration. The group's slogan, United We Stand, was representative of its outlook: at least half of its active members were Latino, and language issues did not cause problems. The Cluster encouraged Latino parents to participate in local activities, and community members considered it a rare integrative force. State Representative Ruiz, who was involved with the Cluster, said:

The Cluster was used as the mechanism, the medium, to get the two groups together. And to—you know, there's always fear in change, resentment in change. And if there isn't a vehicle there to help the transition, then it's going to be antagonistic. And I think that's where, in the field of education, the Cluster was used as the vehicle to bring about the change, and to let people know: don't be afraid, there's nothing to be afraid of. We can all work together. And it worked very well.

Yet despite the breadth of its goals, from enhancing tutoring programs to opening a community center, the Cluster met with success primarily by organizing protests against busing. One local principal noted, "They have a lot of support because they have a single issue [busing]. They tried to be something for everybody . . . And I think . . . they're [becoming] stronger because everyone is focused."

The Cluster attracted support from all levels of the community. Four principals and at least two representatives from every school in Dover and neighboring McAdam Park attended one meeting to elect new board members. All schools with delegates present pledged their support for the anti-busing agenda—except for the magnet school, as one of the Cluster's key goals was to restore local control of that school building. State Representative Ruiz offered his support and said that two Latino state senators also backed the group, and the Cluster maintained ties to local aldermen, the school district, and the Board of Education.

Attendees at Cluster meetings constantly replayed the

themes of unity and cooperation. Comments of the flamboy-ant Italian American male principal of Dover's high school were typical. He stressed that the Board of Education had historically moved only when communities showed solidar-ity, and reiterated that the board must hear "one loud voice" on overcrowding. And anti-busing advocates clearly realized that Latino and white participants must speak with a single voice. In stark contrast to other organizations, in this case the white leadership actively recruited Latinos, took special care to accomodate Spanish-speaking as well as English-speaking members, and framed issues to appeal to Latinos.

PROMOTING LATINO IDENTITY

While the desire to address busing generated interdepen-dence between whites and Latinos, the growing size of the Latino population also created an incentive for political lead-ers to promote ethnic solidarity among Latinos. Besides providing Spanish-language translations during school meet-ings, for example, Lanie Green—the Anglo principal at Ellison Elementary, the neighborhood's most overcrowded school—framed overcrowding as discrimination. She and other school officials invited Representative Ruiz and two Latino state senators to answer questions about overcrowd-ing, and convinced the Mexican American Legal Defense and Education Fund (MALDEF) that it was an ethnic issue. MALDEF responded by taking legal action against the Chicago Board of Education, charging discriminatory treat-ment of Latino communities.

To bolster Latino attendance at a special LSC meeting on the lawsuit, Principal Green invited guest speakers to talk about Latino issues in the schools and the community, and well over a hundred people, mostly Mexican mothers, attended. Throughout the meeting, state representatives stressed the importance of uniting with other Latino communities, citing statistics showing that such districts tended to be the most overcrowded and portraying overcrowding as discrimination rather than the result of changing demographics.

These leaders also discussed voting as a means of personal empowerment, and often offered voter registration at public meetings. A representative from MALDEF commented on the role of ethnic identity in solving the overcrowding problem:

> This is a twenty-year-old problem, but the difference is now we have representatives of our very own to help us. We have Ruiz, Carlos, [and] MALDEF is on top of this. We are working with Carlos and Ruiz, and I also spoke to [Senator] Jose [Alvarez] this morning. He is also anxious to help. That is one of the great benefits of having representatives you can call your own.

Spanish-language newspapers similarly framed stories about overcrowding as discrimination against Latinos. According to one editorial from a local Latino newspaper, "We have 40 to 50 kids in a classroom. Next year they'll be taking the library and the computer room. This is how they discriminate against our kids."[9] The editorial strongly encouraged attendance at the next district meeting on overcrowding and listed the telephone number of the committee chair—a Latino resident of Dover also involved in the LSC and the Cluster.

White principals whose schools served significant numbers of Latinos and politicians anxious to get more Latinos to vote cast Latino interests as being in competition with those of poor black residents of Stockton, and as distinct from those of white Doverites as well. For example, State Representative Ruiz referred explicitly to overcrowding as a struggle between blacks and Latinos over scarce educational resources, maintaining, "We're vying for the same resources that the African American community has laid claim to." Queried about funds earmarked for new schools, Ruiz responded:

It's a political hotbed because you have your white ethnic politicians, who certainly don't want to antagonize either of the minority groups; and you have some of your Hispanic elected officials, who've been in this political arena longer than I have, who have strong ties to the African American community. I particularly— I'm not siding with anyone. I mean, my responsibility is to represent my community in the best way. Whether they're African American, Hispanic, white ethnic, it doesn't matter to me . . . Unfortunately there are limited resources. And we, being the Hispanics, are the fastest-growing minority. We're in desperate need of those resources. Yet there are other groups that want to block it from happening.

ANTI-BLACK SENTIMENT

If there was a commonality between Latinos and whites in Dover, it had to do with their response to African Americans. Latino residents of Dover, including recent arrivals, were no more amenable to living with African Americans than were residents of Eastern European descent. Racism in Dover was exacerbated by the fact that many residents of the nearby black community were destitute, so knowledge about African Americans drawn from adjacent areas reinforced the stereotype of black poverty. In a city well known for its ethnic neighborhoods, residents are very sensitive to the movement of racial and ethnic groups. The "dividing line" between black and nonblack communities is thin, demarcated by wedged Latino enclaves that buffer the two sides. Our study found that aside from city workers such as bus drivers, librarians, and postal workers, few African Americans held jobs in Dover, or even passed casually through the neighborhood.

Residents of both white and Latino areas of Dover often volunteered hostile remarks about African Americans. Although not representative, some white Doverites used the word "nigger" openly in conversation, and did not hesitate to describe their efforts to keep blacks out of the neighborhood as righteous. For example, two whites and one second-generation Latino boasted in a casual street-corner conversation one summer afternoon that the neighborhood was free of "niggers." These men attributed this "success" to the violent reaction of both white and Latino Doverites when African American families moved in.[10]

Of course, residents' words do not always correspond with reality. One older Latino man talked at length about how he enjoyed a bar expressly because it did not serve "niggers," yet directly behind him, not more than ten feet away, sat three middle-aged African American men. While many working-class residents were not shy about using racial epithets, white-collar public servants such as school principals and local and state elected officials were careful to use more neutral language: they emphasized, for example, that they did not want their children bused to schools in "dangerous neighborhoods."

Residents could often be as sophisticated as politicians in making fine distinctions. Lucia, a Mexican American restaurant owner, reported that her younger sister was pregnant and noted that her entire family was very upset because the father of the child was black. Lucia maintained explicitly and adamantly that she did not approve, and that she felt the races should not mix. When Lucia's younger sister teased her about the racism behind her disapproval, she pronounced defiantly, "I am racist!" Yet even though Lucia was a self-proclaimed racist, she appeared to have had no problem dealing with African Americans on a professional basis. Lucia's restaurant sat on a large thoroughfare on the edge of the community, heavily traveled by African Americans, and when black postal workers came in for takeout she treated them with warm familiarity.

No discussion of race would be complete without acknowledging its connection to class. Race is tightly infused with class, and it would be an analytical mistake to discuss race relations in Dover without accounting for the overlap between race and class. Most of the older white residents of Dover lived on fixed incomes. Among these members of the community especially, there was strong support of meritocratic, industrious ideology. Thus Dover residents were generally disdainful of lower-class persons, especially those whom they perceived to be part of the non-working lower class. This notion applied to members of both minority and non-minority communities.

For example, during a local primary election in which State Representative Ruiz ran for alderman, our researchers volunteered as poll watchers, spending the afternoon with three white sisters, the daughters of one of the ward veterans who worked on the Ruiz campaign. The women were working as election judges in charge of recording voters' names and addresses and verifying their signatures. They treated most voters in a congenial manner, but they were noticeably colder—even rude, in our researchers' opinion—to voters who were obviously poor, all of whom were white. For instance, a white man came to vote wearing a slightly torn, dingy overcoat. From his disheveled appearance, he appeared to be homeless. When he told one of the sisters his address, it was clear that he was in the wrong voting district.

Throughout the day, several voters had come to the polling station unsure of their specific district. In these cases, one or all of the sisters would briskly check the person's residential address against a district map of the city and politely direct him or her to the correct polling place. This time, however, all three judges were impolite to the man. Without saying a word, one sister got up to look at the map, leaving the man standing there, confused. She took an inordinate amount of time to look up his address, then told him in an irritated tone the location of his legal polling place. As he walked away, she looked over at some other volunteers, opened her eyes wide, and derisively mouthed the word "scary."

Dover residents were generally unsympathetic to those they perceived as part of the "undeserving" poor, black or white. Nevertheless, they tended to associate poverty with African Americans. The impoverished neighborhoods surrounding Dover are primarily populated by blacks, reinforcing this stereotypical conception of all blacks. These areas are plagued with high rates of adult joblessness, welfare dependence, and crime. Boarded-up shops and other symptoms of urban blight stand in stark contrast to the more attractive Latino and white communities nearby. Such comparisons obviously left an indelible impression on the racial attitudes of Dover residents.

THE FUTURE OF DOVER

Once an area of working-class Eastern European immigrants, Dover's evolution into a haven for Mexican Americans serves as an apt example of a Chicago neighborhood undergoing a recent ethnic transformation. The prevalent response of whites toward the new entrants of Latino descent proved negative. Tensions extended beyond differences in language and culture, but those factors certainly contributed to the lack of understanding between the two groups. Mexicans, resistant to the dilution of their cultural practices, expressed resentment toward white residents, who were generally older and limited in their interaction with the new members of the community. Many whites also argued that the influx of Latinos caused a general rise in crime throughout the neighborhood, further hindering congenial relations.

However, these complaints were not accompanied by actions to resist the ethnic transformation of the neighborhood. In Albert Hirschman's terms, whites resorted to exit, not voice, when they became dissatisfied with changes in their neighborhood. The tipping point that transformed the neighborhood from white ethnic to Latino was reached during the 1990s. The rapid exodus of whites from Dover will very likely continue until they become a negligible percentage of the population.

Unlike Beltway, Dover lacked the institutional strength and the population stability to prevent a rapid ethnic turnover. Dover had been struggling through economic decline prior to the en masse arrival of Mexican Americans. Industrial layoffs, coupled with the exodus of many of the more affluent whites to the suburbs, created housing vacancies that lowered property values. The substantial inmigration of Latinos, many from surrounding Mexican American enclaves, reversed this trend by sharply increasing population density and the demand for housing.

As we have seen, Dover business and civic organizations created and run by whites have been on the path of decline largely due to a reluctance or an inability to draw partici-

pants from the Latino community. Whether an aging or fleeing white population creates vacancies, the result is the same:
these organizations are withering away. Local churches, on
the other hand, have attracted large numbers of Latino members, but cultural clashes have led to ethnic divisions that
generally resulted in the two groups segregating themselves.
None of these developments created situations that would
encourage whites to remain in or maintain loyalty to the
neighborhood, and therefore eschew the exit option.

Despite the ethnic divisions, however, schools have provided a common ground for unification and integration, as
white and Latino parents, faced with the threat of an unap-
pealing solution to overcrowded schools, joined forces in the
battle against busing. Vigorously opposing busing and stress-
ing the need for the construction of new schools, white and
Latino parents argued that the underutilized receiver schools
were inferior and that their location in dangerous neighborhoods placed their children in harm's way. Since the underutilized schools were predominantly black, statements made
about the safety and quality of education cannot be separated
from attitudes about race.

While the need to fight busing as a solution to school
overcrowding generated a sense of interdependence among
whites and Mexican Americans, other incentives fostered the
promotion of ethnic solidarity in the realm of local politics.
As the Latino population has grown, its potential political
power has increased. In order to utilize the power of Latino
political mobilization, we saw in our fieldwork that institutional actors encouraged, reinforced, and maintained the

idea of a distinct Latino identity. School principals, in their fight against overcrowding in the schools, sought to engage Latinos on the issue by arguing that school over-enrollment was a form of discrimination against Mexicans. Elected officials and local leaders likewise associated school overcrowding with discrimination and used the issue to increase Mexican American voter registration and election turnout in their battles for public office.

Given the continued migration of Mexicans to Chicago neighborhoods, Dover will continue to be a prime destination for Latino settlement—especially for the more well-to-do Latinos who can afford the housing costs. Many of these new residents will come from the Mexican enclave of Archer Park.

CHAPTER FOUR

Archer Park

A Taste of Mexico in Chicago

Written with the collaboration of
Erin Augis, Jennifer L. Johnson, and Jennifer Pashup

The community of Archer Park was once known for its rows of working-class homes and its small Bohemian shops. Its once-bustling commercial thoroughfare, just beyond the Chicago Loop, now featured rows of shops specializing in Mexican products such as tacos and tortillas, as well as tropical vegetables, vividly colored women's dresses, and men's cowboy clothing. The centrality of Latino rites of passage was also evident: merchandise included baptismal dresses, First Communion garments, and wedding gowns; photographers, formal-wear shops, and bakers of wedding cakes advertised their services.

The researchers found a district that exuded a distinctly Latin aura, particularly on Saturdays, when the streets were filled with salsa music, brightly colored banners, and swarming crowds of families with children. An array of street vendors sold popsicles (*paletas*), freshly cooked corn (*elotes*), fried pork skins (*chicharrones*), and fresh fruits and vegetables—a sector that provided employment for many undocumented new arrivals. These sellers also prompted controversy: some residents saw them as a convenience, while others viewed them as unsanitary clutter that unfairly competed with legitimate store owners who paid rent.

Archer Park was traditionally a destination for new European immigrants—mostly from Bohemia and other parts of Czechoslovakia—seeking industrial employment. They carved out a community character befitting their customs. The population peaked in 1920 with 84,000 individuals and then steadily declined through the 1960s as many of the area's settlers, responding to improved economic situations, moved to nearby suburbs.

The population decline ended when Mexicans began arriving in significant numbers in the 1970s. Mexicans initially moved to Archer Park from nearby impoverished Pilsen to the northeast, once also a Bohemian stronghold, which in the 1970s became one of the original sites for Mexican settlement in Chicago. Thus Archer Park rapidly transformed from a neighborhood inhabited exclusively by whites to a haven for Mexican Americans. Henri Hernandez, president of the local Chamber of Commerce, proudly described Archer Park as a well-known Mexican community: "[Archer Park] is truly unique. It has the largest concentration of Mexicans in the Midwest . . . If you live, let's say, in Kansas, and you're a Mexican, you know about [Archer Park]."

Numerous public and nonprofit groups provide services and resources to Archer Park residents, including family counseling, assistance with domestic abuse and teen pregnancy, high school equivalency and English-language classes, and job placement and naturalization services. Spanish is the lingua franca of these interactions.

Indeed, Spanish is essentially Archer Park's first language, spoken in homes, among friends, in shops, and on the street. In 2000, 77 percent of residents five years and older spoke Spanish, and as many as 50 percent spoke English "less than very well."[1] One could easily live in Archer Park and conduct all necessary business without any knowledge of English, and thousands of people do. A member of the local school council noted, "Every meeting that we have is primarily in Spanish, and secondarily it's in English."

Nonetheless, language differences may sometimes dampen Latino participation in voluntary civic meetings in which English speakers do play a major role. Translations can be choppy, inconsistent, or delayed, leaving Latino residents unable to communicate their concerns when they meet with English-speaking elected representatives and city and state bureaucrats.

Language differences, we discovered, could also inhibit interaction with the few remaining white residents. Hoping to increase Latino participation in senior services at Pulaski Park, Cornelia, a park supervisor, remarked, "I'm trying to start a Hispanic seniors' club . . . It's especially important for those seniors who don't speak English." One longtime white resident explained that she could not organize a block-club meeting because, she said, "I don't speak Spanish and none of them [her neighbors] speak English."

Moreover, language barriers discouraged some Archer Park residents from investing time and energy in established institutions outside the neighborhood, and thus severed them from resources, power, and authority. Many Spanish-speaking residents involved in civic activities in Archer Park expressed a desire to carry local issues to a larger forum but found communication difficult as they navigated the bureaucracies of the Chicago Public Schools, the Department of Health, and the Park District. Lack of English-language skills also hindered participation in Southwest Side, citywide, and regional political action committees focused on school- and job-related issues.

Furthermore, language barriers aggravated ethnic and racial antagonisms in Archer Park. Unlike in Beltway and Dover, however, such tension did not primarily relate to concerns about the changing ethnic character of the neighborhood. Archer Park has been a Mexican enclave since the 1970s and, as we shall see, showed no signs of an ethnic change.

Still, many remaining whites felt isolated once the vast majority of their friends and kin had died or moved away. As stores, restaurants, community meetings, and the language spoken on Archer Park's streets have become more "Mexican" and less "American," white residents' feelings of isolation have evolved into feelings of loss and bitterness. However, many mourned the loss of the old community while recognizing that ethnic turnover was part of a larger cycle. "It makes me sad," stated Diane Mamik, a white resident of Archer Park for all of her eighty-five years. "I feel so lost.

There is no one here for me now. There is nothing left for me. They [Mexicans] have taken everything. The neighborhood is Spanish now, but that is the way it goes. I had my time here, and now it is their time. That's life. Things change and people move on."

Archer Park whites often claimed that distrust, violence, and crime had undermined a formerly safe, secure, and nurturing community, and many blamed Latinos for the shift. Tara Johnson, a middle-aged woman whose family had resided in Archer Park for eighty-five years, said she now considered the community a dangerous place. "Let me put it to you this way," she proclaimed emphatically: "At night, get out!" Johnson admitted that she was afraid of being "mugged, murdered, or raped," and that she did not allow her children to play outside unsupervised or to walk to school alone.

Johnson's comments closely resembled those of Leslie Holland, an elderly resident of Archer Park since her birth in 1915:

When I was a young woman, I used to [go out] and come home at two or three a.m. I felt perfectly safe . . . [But now] I can do very little to stand up for myself because [the Mexicans] will retaliate. I cannot go for a walk in the neighborhood or go out at night. I am a prisoner in my own home!

Similarly, according to Larry Redman, a longtime white resident of Archer Park and co-owner of a local funeral home:

[Shootings] are an everyday occurrence here. Every once in a while the news comes out here and does a little blurb, but this stuff is everyday. The leftists and the liberals say its Americans' fault the community is falling apart, but it's not! It's them [Mexicans]!!!

State and local government facilitated the growth of Archer Park as a Mexican American enclave when, in 1965, the University of Illinois constructed a branch campus just west of Chicago's central business district. Mayor Richard J. Daley ostensibly chose this site to create a barrier between low-income neighborhoods and downtown.[2] Although the campus primarily displaced Italian Americans, construction also forced a growing Spanish-speaking population to move. Many of those Latinos migrated to Archer Park.

In 2000, 83 percent of Archer Park was Latino (see Figure 4). The white population had declined from 17 percent in 1980 to 6 percent in 1990, and then to a nearly invisible 3.5 percent in 2000. Meanwhile, the African American population—roughly 8 percent in the period from 1970 to 1990—rose to 13 percent in 2000. Almost all the African Americans live in a concentrated and fairly segregated strip near the neighborhood's northern border, adjacent to the poor black neighborhood of Dunston.

A steady stream of immigrants from Mexico counterbalances the sustained movement of upwardly mobile predecessors to suburbs and other Chicago neighborhoods such as Dover. The Mexican population even expanded toward the black fringe of Archer Park during the 1990s, countering common notions that Latinos shy away from African American neighborhoods. Although the small black population of Archer Park nearly doubled from 1980 to 2000, there was no corresponding decrease in the Latino population. In fact, the large Latino population expanded by nearly half during that same period.

FIGURE 4. ARCHER PARK: TOTAL POPULATION
BY RACE AND HISPANIC ORIGIN, 1980–2000

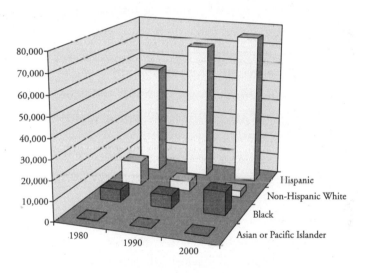

According to the 2000 census, 48 percent of Archer Park residents are "foreign born." Although the census does not specify whether this figure includes undocumented residents, it is nevertheless more than two and a half times the citywide average of 22 percent.[3] Unlike many of their European, Asian, or African counterparts, Mexican immigrants can return home if necessary, and an open migratory circuit between Archer Park and Mexico has allowed people to maintain social ties to their homeland. As one resident put it, this is one of the benefits of "crossing a river, not an ocean." Indeed, the neighborhood's Latino residents—including seasonal workers who sell popsicles on the streets in summer and return to Mexico during the winter—appear to travel often between Mexico and the United States.

This is one reason why many immigrants intended to reside in Archer Park for only a few years, and even longtime residents often refused to relinquish the dream of returning to Mexico. However, many Mexicans who came to Chicago to find jobs and earn money abandoned the desire to leave after their lives took root in the United States. According to one community worker and resident:

> Some of them never plan to stay long in the States or in this neighborhood. Most of them plan on staying one or two years . . . no more than three years. If some of them plan on staying five years, that's a lot. So everybody's thinking to get back to Mexico. They just want to make money and go back. As time passes they realize they're living here ten, fifteen, twenty years. They never go back to Mexico [to live].

When European Americans lived in Archer Park, an emphasis on maintaining the housing stock pervaded the community. Today litter and graffiti—often regarded as by-products of the gang presence—mar the formerly pristine streets. Archer Park officials often confronted the question of why residents did not pour time, energy, and money into the community. However, perceptions of the neighborhood as a temporary haven meant that many residents did not invest in their homes. The principal of a local parochial grammar school explained:

> Mexicans don't think they're going to be living here a long time. That makes them not invest that much in their neighborhood. Like Polish, or even blacks. They . . . are never going back to Africa or the Middle East . . . Every European, when they are going to America, they cut every relationship. It's different. Sometimes Mexicans go back every year and every two years.[4]

Although this respondent simplified the relationship of Europeans and Middle Easterners to their homelands (since between a third and half of eastern and southern Europeans returned home during the first third of the twentieth century),[5] and there were many Mexican American homeowners, his point was that because Mexico is not very far away, people go back and forth frequently, and that movement had consequences for organizational life inside the community. Numerous new arrivals, frequent trips back to Mexico, movement of some middle-class residents to the suburbs, and the organizational preferences for kin—all contributed to sparse formal organizational patterns. For example, efforts to form block clubs foundered in Archer Park. Our researchers observed that sometimes almost nobody showed up at a block-club meeting that had been announced, and those who did were motivated by curiosity to see the inside of a neighbor's house.

Attempts to generate block clubs and other community organizations had a top-down structure. Political figures attempted to organize block clubs for their own organizational purposes. The police department wanted strong block clubs because they put "eyes on the street" and helped officers with crime-control efforts. One such attempt to get people to form block clubs was a "community-wide" meeting held at a local school. Almost all the people who attended were politicians or members of their large entourages, social service providers, representatives of commercial organizations, or parents of children who gave performances to enliven the program. There were even some African Americans who may have been "plants": at various points these individuals stood up to say that block clubs in their neighborhoods had been successful in dealing with crime and keeping the neighborhood cleaned up, and they urged local people to try them. Unfortunately, there were very few actual residents of Archer Park at the meeting.

A staff member at a local park found a similar lack of interest when she tried to organize a Mexican American senior citizens group there. The woman brought her mother to the organizational meeting, but nobody else showed up. Apparently, the park had been trying to organize such a

group for seven years, as a counterpart to a similar seniors
group of ethnic whites.

There were also citywide organizations like UNO, and
even nationwide organizations like ACORN, whose community organizers were trying to instigate community-based
activity through protests. ACCION International, head-
quartered in Washington, D.C., had been trying to provide
economic credit to Archer Park residents who wanted to start
or grow locally based businesses. Even when people were giving things away, though, organized activity came from the
top down and did not necessarily draw a crowd. In a telling
example, a city government–organized neighborhood festival
at a local park served hamburgers and hot dogs instead of
Mexican food. The few neighborhood people who attended
brought their own tacos, tamales, and the like with them.

The paucity of community organizational life and the
absence of local leadership were illustrated by one important
set of meetings to deal with Archer Park issues. These meetings took place not in Archer Park but eight miles away,
at the top of the First National Bank (First Chicago) building downtown. At one typical meeting, bankers from the
community, a representative from the police department, a
representative from one of the Catholic churches, school
principals, social workers, and parole officers met to discuss
such community problems as neighborhood policing and
juvenile gangs.

Fewer than half the people at that meeting had Hispanic
surnames, and the gang-control program that operated out
of the University of Chicago had hired one of those who did.

The meeting illustrated the fact that the people who seemed most concerned about the community were professional and service providers who did not live there, but were there in their professional roles rather than as concerned citizens.

Meetings could be held downtown at the start of the working day because, in effect, people were being paid to attend them. In this sense, these gatherings were quite different from meetings of groups of volunteers, which normally took place in the evening after work. The meetings were held in Chicago's largest bank because its management needed to demonstrate to bank regulators that it was fulfilling the mandates of the Community Reinvestment Act, which requires banks to invest in low-income communities in their service areas. The bank had a branch in Archer Park and saw economic opportunity in the heated-up market of a community crowded with upwardly mobile immigrants trying to save money for home purchases and businesses (often the home purchases and business activities were related). The Archer Park branch catered to Mexican Americans from the entire region, who visited the neighborhood on weekends, and were viewed as potential bank customers.

There was a vast array of paid service providers in the neighborhood. There were programs for pregnant women, and others to work on problems of parenting. There was a program to deal with AIDS. There were general programs related to the delivery of health services, as well as a mental-health clinic. There was a school for at-risk youth, and clubs such as a boys and girls club for youth not particularly at risk. There were gang-prevention programs. There were at least two programs for seniors. There was a branch of a downtown college, programs to deliver GEDs, and programs to teach English to prepare people to become citizens.

Neighborhood Housing Services helped to make housing available and to organize assistance for first-time home buyers. ACCION International made loans to people with either small businesses or entrepreneurial plans. There were, of course, the usual representatives of the state, such as those who ran the schools and the police. And, finally, there were two Chambers of Commerce. Obviously, such an array of service organizations might vitiate the need for local people to organize to help themselves.

This is not to suggest that there was no indigenous organization; it is just that organizations created for people as interest groups or political groups had difficulty getting started. By contrast, kinship and kinship-like structures were pervasive as the primary mode of organization. Outside of kinship networks, many people neither knew their neighbors nor cared much about knowing them. As one respondent reported, "They [neighbors] are not aware of what is happening between families." Entering with them into an instrumental organization was not an automatic choice. Instead, kin served both expressive and instrumental functions, each of which reinforced the other. Networks of kin provided or found places for family members to live, found jobs, offered babysitting, provided transportation to clinics for medical care and to shopping malls, and encouraged participation in important collective rituals, which were family and family-like reinforcements such as christenings, *quinceañeras,* and weddings. Many residents had siblings and cousins living nearby but not usually on the same block, and older residents had children who helped look after them.

POPULATION GROWTH
AND SHRINKING PUBLIC RESOURCES

Destitution resided just under the shell of the community's prosperity and gaiety, as immigrants often lived in unsafe, crowded, subdivided housing, with the men and sometimes the women working long hours at minimum-wage jobs. Although the population of Chicago as a whole declined between 1970 and 1990, Archer Park's population grew 27 percent, and expanded by an additional 12 percent by 2000. Even single-family homes in Archer Park were crowded. Whereas in 1970 the neighborhood reflected the city average of some three persons per household, in 2000 the average number of people per household in Archer Park had expanded to 4.15, compared with a citywide figure of 2.67.[6]

This rapid rise in population density strained local institutions and resources. As the school district superintendent observed:

Overcrowding . . . affects just about everything. There's overcrowding in the residential patterns and . . . in the schools, and that creates crime and poverty and everything else . . . The schools are overcrowded, and that impacts on the upbringing of the children, creating, then, a gang problem because the children feel alienated by the system. But also there is a lot of poverty in the area. There are a lot of immigrants . . . undocumented and documented . . . The community does its best . . . The entire area is overpopulated, and that taxes all the resources available.

Unfortunately, Archer Park's rapid population growth also occurred amid drastic cuts in public spending that began in 1980 and continued unabated into the 1990s. In April 1994, the director of a neighborhood youth recreation club said:

Lately we have undergone major funding cutbacks, which have really negatively affected us programmatically. Normally our budget is about $300,000 to keep the place going for a year. We've just been cut by about $140,000 of that, so we'll be losing quite a few staff. And if you look at the number of kids that we serve here, we have a membership of 1,100 . . . which is difficult when you don't have very many people to work with them.

Residents' incomes had also declined. Median family income in Archer Park was $34,905 in 1979 (in constant 1999 dollars), but twenty years later it had dropped to $32,317.[7] And the poverty level had risen: in 1969 only 12 percent of residents were poor by national standards, but by 1999, 24 percent of the community lived in poverty—seven percentage points higher than that for all of Chicago.[8]

Contractions in public resources, Archer Park's burgeoning population, and rising poverty contributed to a plethora of problems in the neighborhood. According to residents and community leaders alike, these included not only difficulties in maintaining the housing stock but also a proliferation of youth gangs, inadequate police protection, and a lack of neighborhood cohesion. Severe space constraints particularly plagued the neighborhood's public schools; some even converted utility rooms to classrooms. During the mid-1990s Archer Park was home to so many students under the age of twelve that the Chicago Board of Education built five new elementary schools in response to the demands of parents and administrators.[9]

Even with these new schools, however, the director of local group that targets school overcrowding reported that public schools could not adequately meet the community's educational needs. Alderman Carlos Domingues concurred, adding:

> I graduated from Pearl Buck Grammar School in 1979. It was crowded then and it's crowded now. You have schools that are designed for about 1,400 students, now have approximately 2,000 students. Some that were designed for 700 might have 1,200 students . . . When that happens, you don't have room for computer labs, you don't have room for science labs, because every room you get you want to use for basic instruction.

Indeed, as immigrants continue to pour into Archer Park, problems involving space will only mount. As we shall soon see, some of the problems of space undermined intergroup relations in the neighborhood.

In contrast to Beltway and Dover, where the sources of intergroup tensions for the most part have been related to notions of preserving the neighborhood, racial and ethnic antagonisms did not seem to influence social organization in Archer Park. The neighborhood showed no signs of impending ethnic change, and Mexicans appeared firm in their ownership of community institutions.

Although neighborhood preservation underlay ethnic antagonisms during the rapid Mexican influx in the 1970s, now that Archer Park was a Latino enclave, the community's few remaining whites saw little chance of reversing its composition. As one white longtime Archer Park resident put it, "When you got a little money, that's what you did you moved up and out to Seneca. Nobody blames them for leaving; that's just what everybody did."

Because Latinos had claimed most properties, businesses, and institutions in Archer Park, the Mexican population viewed whites as no real threat. One Latina joked, "Yeah, we finally got all of those Bohemians out! Now we can do what we want in the neighborhood." Similarly, although Mexicans were aware of the growing black presence in Archer Park and many expressed anti-black sentiments, these feelings did not stem from fears that blacks seriously challenged Mexican control of Archer Park.

Even the schools were devoid of ethnic competition for enrollment. Indeed, controlled enrollment not only restricted the busing in of students from other communities, it also prohibited the schools from accepting additional students, even when they lived within a school's geographic boundaries, including African American children who lived in the neighborhood. Enrollment of black children—whose families clustered on the community's northern border—declined in nearly all Archer Park schools in the 1990s. Because the few remaining white residents of Archer Park were older and their children tended to be past school age, public schools served the neighborhood's youthful Mexican population almost exclusively. Even schools with white principals and mixed-race faculty seemed to maintain a Latino identity.

The city often relied on busing to address severe overcrowding. Thomas Rose, principal of Walton Grammar School, explained, "We have a bit of a problem with mobility because of the fact that we're under controlled enrollment, which means that we can't take in everybody who comes because we have a limited amount of space." Asked where Archer Park children would end up going to school, Principal Rose responded, "They are then transferred to a school that has space . . . It could be as far away as three, four, five miles."

However, unlike in Dover, during the time of our research, busing had not provoked controversy or dominated community forums such as the local school council, in part because Chicago Public Schools authorities maintained a policy of busing students in predominantly Latino schools to other Latino schools if space was available.[10] Still, the probability that Archer Park students would attend other Latino schools was shrinking as overcrowding became more severe, and busing would undoubtedly become more of an issue among Latino parents, especially those with children bused to predominantly black schools. According to a spokesperson for the CEO of Chicago Public Schools: "In cases of over-crowding in predominantly Latino schools, we try to send them to other Latino schools if there is availability. However, the probability of finding excess space in predominantly Latino schools is low. It is likely that students residing within the attendance areas of predominantly Latino schools on controlled enrollment will be bused to non-Latino schools."[11]

RACE AND NEIGHBORHOOD
SOCIAL ORGANIZATION

Mexicans in Archer Park were not preoccupied with discrimination. At public meetings, residents raised concerns about crime, for example, but did not accuse police of practicing ethnic discrimination or of providing inferior services because the community was largely Latino. In contrast, at a block-club summit for the ward containing Archer Park, residents from the adjacent African American community of Dunston invoked race as a key factor in the perceived lack of police zeal in combating crime. When Latino residents felt that African Americans' focus on race took attention away from their concerns about controlling crime, they openly voiced their displeasure.

Interestingly, groups dedicated to ethnic-specific Latino issues were notably absent from Archer Park. A few local organizations claimed to pursue public policy and legal issues in the best interests of Latinos, but they did not appear to be highly regarded or widely supported. Chapters or offshoots of larger organizations, these groups brought national agendas to Archer Park rather than devoting themselves to local issues, and retained outsider status in a neighborhood where kin and personal relationships were critical.

During the mid-nineties a few politicians visited Archer Park to have their pictures taken or to support Latino issues, such as opposition to California's Proposition 187, which eliminated public services for illegal immigrants and their children. These visits and speeches did not elicit much excitement or support, however—even during close elections. Residents might view organizations dedicated to Latino issues as unnecessary because Mexicans composed the majority of most formal organizations. The absence of organizations devoted to Latino issues might also reflect residents' unwillingness to make long-term commitments to the community. In fact, deep connections to Mexico often meant that residents professed little desire to form close ties and join local organizations.

If racial and ethnic antagonisms were not a salient feature of the social organization of Archer Park within the specifically Mexican enclave—that is, where the Latino ownership of institutions and organizations was clearly established—such antagonisms did mar relations among Mexicans, whites, and African Americans when the groups openly competed for access to public recreational space and facilities located in areas that were mainly on the periphery rather than in the center of Archer Park. Neighborhood overcrowding and shrinking public resources exacerbated these conflicts.

Because both organized and impromptu sports teams and clubs often had ethnically and racially homogeneous membership, residents viewed competition for scarce recreational space as an ethnic and racial struggle. Recreational facilities were in short supply; most were open for only a few hours each day because managers could not afford to pay full-time workers. One director of a local boys and girls club explained:

The federal budget cuts really hurt us a couple years back. We need to hire staff, but we just can't afford to pay them. And we can't count on volunteers to keep coming back. We have 1,300 kids here at this club, and we see about 200 to 300 kids a day. But we can only afford to stay open a few hours each day. Like the swimming pool? We can only open it on Wednesday, Thursday, and Friday, because we can't afford more lifeguard time.

Competition for public recreational space provoked conflict particularly between African American and Mexican teenagers, as each group wanted access to baseball diamonds and basketball courts. Park directors forced the two groups to alternate their use of such facilities, and youths admitted to taking verbal and physical steps to make the "other group" feel unwelcome as they stood around waiting to use park space and equipment. One such incident occurred between teens participating in Pathways, a local group that offered family counseling, a shelter for runaway teens, adult education, and an alternative high school for teenage dropouts. At the beginning of 1995, Pathways received a grant from the Clinton administration's AmeriCorps to foster understanding among youth from different ethnic and racial backgrounds. Since the grant stipulated that organizational recipients could create programs based on the specific needs of their communities, Pathways administrators chose to focus on the integration of local recreational facilities, which were largely segregated by ethnic group.

At that time, facilities in the northern section of Archer Park were dominated by African American teens, while Mexicans primarily used the central and southern sections of the park. Pathways hired college-age youths to lead groups of Mexican and African American teens to each other's field houses and organize joint games. Despite these efforts, one Pathways official noted that relations between the groups were so combative that the youths fought constantly and engaged in a good deal of "nigger-spic name-throwing."

Adults using public facilities also evinced ethnic and racial tensions. One Chicago Park District official reported that a Mexican church group moved Bible-study sessions to her facility because they felt threatened by African American youth: "[Mexicans] used to hold meetings at [Jackson Park], which is all black . . . There were lots of problems with people's chains and stuff getting ripped off, so now they hold them at [a predominantly Mexican park], and they feel safer."

Regular skirmishes also occurred between Mexican park

users and members of the seniors' club, which was dominated by people of Polish and Czech descent, at Pulaski Park, situated on Archer Park's southern border. The seniors club had exclusive use of the largest room in the park's recreation building. The conflict occurred because there were not enough rooms for all the groups who wished to use Pulaski Park to conduct their meetings; meanwhile, the members of the seniors club were determined to retain control over their only space. Mexican users of the park were eager to have access to the large room; they resented the lack of space they were allotted in the recreation building, and were critical of the seniors group's exclusive use of the room. Thus, group competition for public space was translated into ethnic competition between Latinos and whites.

Except for the ethnic tensions manifested in the competition for public recreational space outside the central areas of Archer Park, ethnic antagonisms tended not to be reflected in neighborhood social organization. Neither blacks nor whites posed any serious threat to Mexican dominance. Aside from a lack of a perceived threat to Mexican dominance in Archer Park, the relatively lower commitment to the neighborhood as a permanent place of residence also decreased concerns about the future of the neighborhood and its institutions, or of ethnic or racial changes in the neighborhood.

What did concern the Mexican population of Archer Park was their relative status vis-à-vis African Americans. Unlike in Beltway and Dover, where hostility toward blacks was associated with neighborhood preservation and access to and control of local public schools, Mexican animus toward African Americans in Archer Park involved attempts to differentiate themselves from blacks in terms of social prestige. This was accomplished in two main ways: Mexicans explicitly described the actions of African Americans as socially unacceptable, in their desire to escape the stigmas of poverty and criminal activity routinely ascribed to minorities such as blacks and Latinos in the United States; and many Mexicans interviewed by our field-workers even more explicitly set themselves apart from African Americans by commenting on the undesirability of dark skin or of "looking black."

Because Latinos in Archer Park faced constraints on opportunity and upward mobility, such as unemployment and poor schools, they expressed intense concern about their social status, and relied on stereotypical stories and views to contrast themselves with African Americans.[12] Mexican residents took pains to characterize blacks as people who acted in ways that deviate from community norms, and made clear their conviction that they would behave quite differently in similar circumstances.

For example, Archer Park Mexicans often associated local African Americans with theft. An ice cream vendor maintained that he never sold in the black neighborhoods surrounding Archer Park because "they [blacks] will rob you." A block-club president and his wife claimed that African Americans were stealing appliances from their neighbors. Another couple, Vincente and Marta, talked about *el prietito*—the little black man who had been stealing things from people on their street. Vincente recounted a day when he brought ladders upstairs from his cellar. According to Vincente, the ladders had disappeared within a few minutes, and he considered the black man the obvious culprit. Marta added that she had noticed *la prieta,* the black woman, wheeling a television set out of a neighbor's house in a wheelbarrow, and she said that the black man was waiting on the sidewalk to escort the woman. The couple also mentioned that another neighbor had recently purchased an ice cart that had been stolen soon after, and that blacks had been blamed.

Marino, the owner of Hyde Street, a local diner, regularly warned customers about the "dangerous" parts of the neighborhood, advising travelers to avoid Long Street because "it's black." Characterizing these areas as perilous and crime-ridden, he admonished one field-worker to avoid public-transit stops, as they were frequented by African Americans. Young Mexicans also volunteered their perceptions of African Americans as criminally inclined. One high school student advised her peers to "watch out for the blacks" if they were going to ride the West Street bus.

These responses reflected a genuine fear of crimes allegedly perpetrated by African Americans against the Mexican community. However, such accounts also reflected a sentiment—pervasive in American society—that associates people of color with poverty, violence, and crime. Because such views threatened their own status and social well-being, Mexicans attempted to distinguish themselves from a group perceived as even more economically disadvantaged and stigmatized.

Many Archer Park Mexicans characterized African Americans as unruly and disrespectful, with several basing their perceptions on experiences with African Americans who acted in "objectionable" ways. For example, restaurant owner Marino scolded an African American woman who entered his establishment asking for money. After he threw her out, he talked about other experiences he had had with "those people." According to Marino, a black man had entered his restaurant the previous summer and "lay right on the counter," demanding—with hostility—a glass of water. Marino said he went back to the kitchen, picked up a knife, and told the man to leave immediately. He continued, "And then he had the nerve to flag a cop car! The cop came to talk to me—and I know this cop—and he asked my why I had to use a knife to get the guy out of here. I said if I hadn't he would have been back in the kitchen by then!"

There is no doubt that when Latinos and African Americans interacted, contrasting social mannerisms intensified intergroup tensions. Silvia, one of the waitresses at Hyde Street, asserted that African Americans were generally rude, calling black women "bitches" in a whispered conversation. Silvia said that once, an African American couple in their early forties had entered the restaurant and walked up to the counter. According to Silvia, the woman asked the price of a can of soda in a "curt manner." Just as curtly, Sylvia stated that the small cans were seventy-five cents and the large bottles were a dollar. Without further comment, the African American woman turned around to leave, saying in a disgusted voice, " 'Shhhh,' like 'shit.' "

Mexican residents also complained about unpleasant encounters with black city employees. One field-worker reported a confrontation between a Latino passenger and an African American bus driver who refused to accept a transfer because he said it had expired. When the rider tried to explain that a full hour had not yet elapsed, the driver became unpleasant, almost abusive. Others on the bus, checking their watches, agreed with the passenger.

Such encounters presented a dilemma for upwardly striving Mexican immigrants. Many considered themselves socially superior to blacks, yet they believed African Americans had firm holds on lower-level government jobs. This enhanced blacks' power in interacting with Latinos regarding services such as public transportation, Social Security, welfare, public parks, and libraries. Mexicans often felt insulted by black officials, who frequently claimed they could not understand Latinos' accented English, and many blacks shared with many European whites a sense of superiority over lower-status residents who had difficulty speaking English. Mexicans found it irritating that the behavior of African Americans seemed to reflect this feeling; poor Mexicans who lacked English skills were especially resentful.

In Archer Park, many Latinos deliberately set themselves apart from African Americans by commenting on how undesirable it was to "look black." Some Mexicans identified individuals with dark skin as indigenously Indian, with little or no white ancestry, while others associated dark skin with "being black." The point was clear in either case: dark skin implied low social standing and undesirability in American society.

Mexican youth often discussed the disadvantages of having dark skin. At a local high school, a seventeen-year-old student volunteered that the reason she did not participate in outdoor activities was because she did not want her skin to "get dark." One sixteen-year-old reported that he could not set his friend up with girls because the friend was "too chocolate." And a dark-toned Mexican student retorted to teasing peers, "I'm not black!"

While Mexican teenagers might be overly sensitive to the social disadvantages of dark skin, adults, too, acknowledged that dark skin was considered less prestigious and often associated dark-skinned Mexicans with poverty.[13] One close-knit family of grown siblings joked about their mother's complexion. Her son-in-law teased, "Oh, you'd better turn the lights up in here when she comes in! . . . All her kids are light as snow, but she's very dark." He went on to identify darkness with being African American by describing his mother-in-law as "dark" and "ugly" with a "big, wide, black nose."

Exceptions to these racial and ethnic antagonisms did exist, however. In the mid-1990s, the Chicago Community Trust awarded the Chicago Public Schools $325,000 to beautify schools with educational art, and Archer Park's Lawson School received funding for a mural project. The section of the mural pertaining to African American history and art equaled that of the portion devoted to Latino culture. Considering that the vast majority of students at the school were Latino, teachers appeared to be making a concerted effort to include African American culture in their classrooms. Our field-workers also observed a number of friendships between

Mexicans and blacks in Archer Park, even among residents who made ethnically inflammatory statements.

Overall, however, Archer Park sheds light on the dynamics of intergroup relations in a neighborhood where ethnic control of key institutions is firmly established. Latinos faced a quandary in deciding whether to self-identify—or allow others to codify them—as an oppressed minority group. The forms of the 2000 U.S. Census allowed Latinos to choose "white" as a racial identity while specifying Hispanic origin as an ethnic identity. Many Latinos resisted both white and nonwhite racial classifications, instead labeling themselves "other."[14] Minority status may sometimes appeal to Latinos because they can gain access to social benefits and programs aimed at redressing discrimination. Yet foreign-born Latinos are often more comfortable calling themselves immigrants than appending themselves to America's ever-growing list of "minorities." Immigrant status links Latinos' experience with that of European Americans and their immense pride in their "courageous forefathers." Immigrant status also allows Latinos to tap into the American melting-pot ideal and ethos of upward mobility based on ambition, self-discipline, and hard work.[15]

A "STEPPING-STONE" COMMUNITY

Archer Park reached a tipping point in the 1970s, when the neighborhood transitioned from white Bohemian to Latino. Since then the neighborhood has shown no sign that its Latino dominance is threatened. Archer Park remains a strong Mexican enclave because of the continuous in-migration of individuals and families from Mexico. Just as one Mexican family departs the neighborhood, another Mexican family replaces it.

Partly for this reason, during our study, issues of race and ethnicity were no longer a salient aspect of the social organization of the neighborhood. There was no perceived need for Mexicans to align themselves against either blacks or whites. However, Archer Park is unique for another reason. Of the four neighborhoods in this study, Archer Park was most distinct in its status as a "stepping-stone" community. For example, Dover, which ranked above Archer Park in terms of housing prices and class status, included many Mexican residents who once lived in Archer Park.[16]

Our field researchers observed signs of transience rather than permanence in Archer Park, a view confirmed by the remarks of most residents who aspired to move. Further-more, even longtime Archer Park residents exhibited feelings of longing for another community. Accordingly, aside from the absence of a perceived threat to Mexican dominance in Archer Park, the relatively lower commitment to the neighborhood as a permanent place of residence decreased concerns about the future of the neighborhood and its institutions.

To repeat, given the continuous flow of Mexicans to Archer Park, the high proportion of residents who exited neither affected nor changed the ethnic makeup of the neighborhood. There was no need to resort to voice—that is, to take active steps—to preserve Mexican dominance. In short, except for the small group of remaining older whites in the neighborhood, the desire to exit and the lack of loyalty to Archer Park had little to do with concerns about neighborhood racial or ethnic transformation.

Nonetheless, as we have seen, anti-racial sentiments did exist. Mexicans in Archer Park were concerned about their status vis-à-vis African Americans and felt that they must work hard to differentiate themselves from blacks.

The widespread feeling of racial competition in the larger city of Chicago also pervaded Archer Park. Although there was little racial competition within Archer Park itself, the Mexicans believed that they were competing with African Americans for scarce resources in the larger city, and they furthermore concluded that blacks had already received an unfair share of these resources. They would probably not hesitate to cite the large proportion of city workers in the black neighborhood of Groveland to support this claim.

CHAPTER FIVE

Groveland

A Stable African American Community

Written with the collaboration of
Reuben A. Buford May and Mary Pattillo

A frican Americans migrated from the South to Chicago's racially segregated "Black Belt" from 1950 through 1970 and garnered a higher share of local jobs. As a result, the city's South Side became ever more African American.[1] The predominantly white community of Groveland proved no exception to this dramatic expansion of the black community. Only 6 of 12,710 Groveland residents enumerated in the 1960 census were African American. A decade later, blacks accounted for 83 percent of Groveland residents, and by 1990 the neighborhood's black population had reached 98 percent.

Real estate speculators helped fuel this rapid racial displacement. Capitalizing on strong demand for housing by both blacks and whites, these deceitful speculators staged episodes of violence to convince white residents that African Americans were bringing crime and drugs into Groveland.

In October 1959 three white *Chicago Daily News* jour-
nalists highlighted the real estate sharks—both black and
white—who preyed on Groveland homeowners. "The Panic-
Peddlers," a nine-part exposé, included the names and addresses, as well as photographs, of these "blockbusters" who
used intimidation and terror to induce whites into selling
their homes quickly and cheaply. Although local civic organizations attempted to preserve racial diversity in Groveland, the speculators triumphed: homes were resold at
escalated prices to African Americans.

Fifty-year-old Al Charles, who grew up in the post–
World War II Black Belt, recalled how venturing into Groveland was then a perilous enterprise,[2] as white children would
beat up black youngsters who crossed Chicago's symbolic
Mason-Dixon line. "I always had to have some friends go
with me, and we had better be prepared to fight."

Charles and his adventuresome friends formed the van-
guard that presaged the expansion of the Black Belt. Infre-
quent youthful trips into white neighborhoods preceded
waves of migration by entire families to South Side neighborhoods, and later into select suburbs that eventually became
black enclaves. Akeem Davis, an African American in his forties who moved into the neighborhood when he was a
teenager, remarked: "When I first moved here, the neighborhood was going through racial changes. I remember you
would walk out of the house and get jumped on. There were
other ethnic groups and sometimes we couldn't walk down
the street without getting pop bottles thrown at us." Despite
these incidents, Groveland proved relatively immune to the

violence endemic to other Chicago neighborhoods during the period of racial turnover, as white residents largely avoided tactics designed to stave off an influx of blacks. While whites expressed concern about losing their familiar neighborhood, those with economic resources simply relocated to newer suburbs built soon after World War II. As one longtime resident of Groveland noted, "For the most part, white people just quietly moved. They didn't say anything; they just left."[3] By 1970 the process of racial turnover was nearly complete.

Groveland did not succumb to widespread violence for several reasons. First, since it was situated nearly six miles from the original Black Belt, Groveland did not receive a large in-migration of African Americans until halfway through the 1960s. Second, the relatively high social and economic standing of longtime white homeowners and incoming African Americans alike smoothed the process of racial change. In fact, new black residents actually held a slight economic and educational edge over the neighborhood's previous occupants. Residents' median years of schooling rose from 12.1 to 12.4 years from 1960 to 1970, for example, while their poverty rate fell from 6.1 to 5.1 percent.

Incoming African Americans also had much in common with white residents, as Groveland's brick-faced, suburban-style, single-family homes appealed to families who preferred to buy rather than rent. Thus landlords could not exploit the fast-paced housing market by subdividing apartments for blacks with lower incomes. Because of these influences, the proportion of homeowners in Groveland has remained above

70 percent since 1950, and many residents have lived in the neighborhood for decades.[4]

African American residents often arrived in Groveland from neighborhoods where congested buildings in disarray and streets soiled with litter lowered property values and fostered crime. These new residents exhibited a vigorous desire to maintain their new dwellings. A visit to Groveland revealed the fruits of this desire for cleanliness and neighborhood upkeep, as signs reading WELCOME and billboards urging HAVE A NICE DAY! framed finely landscaped houses.[5] Residents actively encouraged car owners to drive slowly and mind children who might be playing in the neighborhood. This community spirit manifested itself in other ways as well. According to Melissa Rains, a staff member for the alderman representing Groveland, residents who lived near a group of abandoned houses "all come together and mow the lawn and pick up the trash so that you really can't tell that the houses are abandoned."

Block clubs—the neighborhood's most visible form of social organization—played a critical role in ensuring that newcomers observed traditions established by older members of the community and provided a venue for neighbors to deal collectively with their problems. Block-club signs such as DRIVE CAREFULLY, NO LOUD MUSIC, NO LITTERING, and NO HORN BLOWING adorned the entrances to many areas, reflecting the middle-class status of residents who remained vigilant lest low-income patterns of behavior emerge. Alderman Trisha Hill reported that block clubs effectively addressed two central issues in Groveland, graffiti and sanitation, as the clubs invited representatives from city departments to meet with their members. Block clubs also advanced proposals for combating crime, paving streets, putting up Christmas lighting, and removing sidewalk snow. Overall, the block clubs "are very effective in rendering city services," according to Hill.

Longtime residents had built strong families and lasting friendships around their shared concern for the neighborhood's future. Linda Marshall, a thirty-eight-year-old married mother of two, lived with her husband, whom she met in high school, within a block of both their parents. Three of Linda's five sisters resided nearby with their children, and another sister had recently moved to a neighborhood in the immediate vicinity. Linda reflected on the neighborhood's close relationships:

> You'd never know it, but it's like one big family around here. Like if you just came up here [to the Groveland field house], you'd never know all the people that's related, like Diedra and Bird and Lance are brothers and sisters. And like Spider went to Jackson [High School] with Julie [her sister]. They used to share a locker . . . 'Cause, see, I live on this block and my mother lives on this block and then Moe's mama [her mother-in-law] lives on this block.

Plummeting demand for low-skilled workers stemming from deindustrialization left many black neighborhoods in Chicago with few employment opportunities, but Groveland remained insulated from these structural economic changes.[6] In fact, many adult workers in Groveland benefited from an economic restructuring that favored their higher skills and technical and professional expertise. According to the 1980 census, 59 percent of Groveland's population was employed in white-collar occupations; this figure had risen to 65 percent by 2000. Almost one-third of Groveland's employed population worked for the city, state, or federal government.

Government jobs instilled a sense of control and power among residents that was apparent in casual conversations and at community meetings. Residents often relied on their strong links to government officials to try to rectify problems, typically showing much persistence. At one meeting on public safety, Sara Wilson, a woman in her mid-thirties, complained about a neighbor who was fixing cars and using hazardous materials in the alley near her home. According to Sara, despite two complaints to the city government and a call to 911, no police car had driven past to examine the situation. Even when her husband, a Chicago firefighter, complained within the fire department, nothing happened. Finally her cousin, who worked for the police department, drove through the alley and warned the man, but he continued undeterred. Having first pursued informal routes, Sara arrived at the police beat meeting to formally ask for help, and the police representative assured her that an officer would check out the situation as soon as possible.

Likewise, when the city dispatched officials to address a community meeting, those delegates were likely to be black and familiar to the audience. Leading elected officials lived in the community, and voter turnout was exceptionally high. Groveland residents not only posted the highest voter turnout among our four neighborhoods, they boasted one of the highest voting averages in the city as a whole. And residents did not routinely vote for African American candidates.

Although Groveland had many desirable qualities, including civic engagement, it had not attracted nonblack ethnic groups. While Latinos had flowed into many Chicago neighborhoods, including Beltway, Dover, and Archer Park, over the past decade, Groveland's tiny Latino population of 1 percent remained virtually unchanged from 1990 to 2000. Meanwhile, the white population fell slightly—below 1 percent—while the African American population also declined by 5.4 percent (see Figure 5). This contrasts with our other three neighborhoods, all of which have gained residents since 1990.[7]

Although occasions for interracial contact within Groveland were few, race remained a topic of discussion, as we will see below. But concerns about interracial tensions were often secondary to the project of forging a black identity.

FORGING A BLACK IDENTITY

Most of the action in Spike Lee's 1989 movie *Do the Right Thing* occurred in an Italian American–owned pizzeria in a black neighborhood in Brooklyn. As he pointed to photos of Frank Sinatra, Rocky Marciano, Joe DiMaggio, and other American icons of Italian descent, Buggin Out, one of the main characters, asked the Italian owner, "Sal, why it ain't no

black people up on the wall?" Sal responded that only prominent Italian Americans would ever adorn the walls of *his*
pizzeria.

FIGURE 5. GROVELAND: TOTAL POPULATION BY RACE
AND HISPANIC ORIGIN, 1980–2000

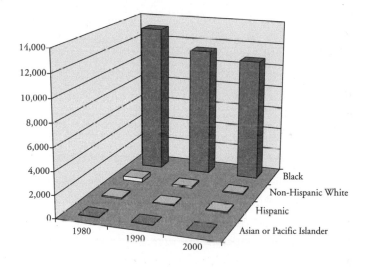

Groveland was similarly replete with images of African
Americans and symbols of black identity. The walls of a recreation room in a building at a local park boasted photographs
and mini-biographies of black heroes such as Frederick
Douglass, Duke Ellington, Michael Jackson, Michael Jor-
dan, Martin Luther King, Jr., Rosa Parks, Harriet Tubman,
Booker T. Washington, and Faye Wattleton. A black-and-

white photo of Malcolm X anchored the collage, surrounded by red, black, and green—colors informally adopted as the African American flag.[8] A portrait of Chicago's first African American mayor, the late Harold Washington, hung in the hallway, and Groveland's library featured an exhibit of portraits of famous African Americans. These photographs expressed the residents' sense of ownership of these institutions.

Posters of black musicians also adorned Groveland's main street, and "Black Is," a poem by a Groveland elementary school student featuring the qualities she associates with being African American—smart, cool, wonderful, beautiful, peaceful, and right—was also on display throughout the neighborhood. Shop windows featured black-oriented merchandise: small bookshops, for example, showcased children's books with black characters on the covers. The entrance to the local Catholic school featured art on the meaning of being black, and church bulletin boards announced Black History Month. An African American flag and kente cloth— a patterned fabric produced in Ghana and worn by members of the African diaspora as a symbol of their continent of origin—formed the backdrop for the altar of the Catholic church.

Groveland residents expressed their identity not only through icons and symbols, but through sound as well. Soul and rhythm and blues often echoed through the neighborhood park, and teenagers played basketball accompanied by rap music on Sundays from March through October. The local day camp concluded its activities by producing a musical featuring the work of black artists, as children danced to songs sung by the audience. At one such recital, teenage camp-goers and attendees joined in caroling the gospel song "Why We Sing."

Residents, business owners, government employees, and church leaders used such symbols to reinforce Groveland's black identity, while the presence of these images throughout the neighborhood contributed to a sense of inclusion in local institutions. Like Archer Park, Groveland was not undergoing a process of neighborhood change, so little disagreement occurred over which symbols were appropriate for public display. This situation contrasts with Dover, where residents cited changing racial and ethnic signifiers within neighborhood institutions as a primary cause of conflict.

Some facets of Groveland's landscape transcended racial significance. Most local homeowners took great pride in the aesthetics of the neighborhood, with some tarring driveways, planting flowers, and trimming bushes, and others hiring professional landscapers to tend lawns and gardens during the summer. Neighbors who carefully trimmed bushes and tended flowers encouraged other neighbors to do the same. In the autumn, residents stuffed leaves into decorative bags, and most celebrated the holiday season with Christmas lights and displays. One young woman commented on her decision to put up a few Christmas decorations: "Everyone else on the block had stuff up, so we figured we better get some stuff."

Timberlin—a section of the neighborhood that boasts newer and larger homes—hosted a holiday decoration contest every December.[9] Winners proudly displayed signs designating their homes and yards as the most attractive and best decorated. In other sections of Groveland, residents pooled money and purchased decorative lampposts to line the edges of their properties. Residents employed these class markers to distinguish their neighborhood from poorer surrounding communities.

The lines that separated Groveland and the rest of society were not roads or train tracks, but rather a prevailing concept of what it means to be African American and—more specifically—a black person living in Groveland. However, unlike in Beltway, where efforts to perpetuate ethnic culture often included verbally attacking people of color, the forging of a black identity in Groveland did not entail overt aversion to whites or other ethnic groups, nor was the proliferation of black symbols a direct response to white racism. Nevertheless, the public expression of black identity did help maintain racial boundaries, as we shall soon see.

GROVELAND'S RELATIVE LACK
OF RACIAL TENSIONS

While the mainstream media provide a bleak commentary on the state of race relations in the United States, casual conversations in Groveland seldom conveyed overt racial and ethnic hatred, or even antagonism. Nor did residents express the "rage of the black middle class," despite their continual references to racial discrimination.[10] In fact, residents recalled mutual neighborliness between whites and blacks even during the period of neighborhood turnover. This behavior stands in sharp contrast to the racial and ethnic attitudes expressed by residents in our other three neighborhoods. Commenting on the lack of racial tension in Groveland, an African American store owner remarked, "We're an inclusive race."

The views of Groveland residents frequently extended beyond sociability to include support for whites in the community. For example, when Ms. Marshall, the white park supervisor, was slated for transfer to another park, residents rallied to keep her in Groveland, calling and writing the Chicago Park District. Residents' positive interactions with Ms. Marshall enabled them to look beyond race, and they ultimately retained her as park supervisor.

Residents were also willing to grant a certain amount of consideration to the feelings of whites. Some planners of a reunion for St. Catherine alumni expressed concern that white attendees might not feel comfortable walking the considerable distance between the parking lot and the school building. The planning committee also felt that the deejay should include mainstream popular music so white alumni would not feel isolated in a room filled mostly with African Americans dancing to black music. (It should be noted, though, that some planners did express resentment about making special efforts to accomodate whites, who were not expected to attend in large numbers anyway.)

Because of Chicago's high rates of residential segregation, residents' exposure to whites and other nonblacks tends to be limited to activities supported by institutions. These include athletic events sponsored by the Chicago Park District, such as the citywide volleyball tournament. Jermaine, a Groveland resident, recalled the athletic skills of a young white player and the positive interactions among players from different parts of Chicago:

> The best player I ever seen was this tall, blond white boy. I use to play over there with Ms. Jackson at Groveland. One year, we made it to the end of the tournament. We was playin' over there, way west. It was a whole buncha Mexicans and Puerto Ricans and stuff, but they was cool. We was like the only team from the South Side that made it that far. So we was playin' and they had these two little dudes up in the front. And they did that settin' stuff . . . Little man in the front went up and faked and then that white boy came from the back outta nowhere. All you saw was him comin' up and the ball flyin' over the net. That boy was bad. After the game, they asked us to stay. They had some burgers and brats [bratwurst] and so we stayed for a while drinking soda and eatin'. They was playin'—what's that shit?—the Rolling Stones. We was chillin'.

Jermaine recalled not only the white player's impressive skill, but also the pleasant interaction among all the groups around volleyball, food, and music. Some teens also reported positive experiences playing basketball with whites. According to one player, "I used to play with this white boy up on the North Side. I was the only black up there. It was cool." At least two members of a group of Groveland teens reported that they had close friends who were white, noting that friends were people they truly trust. One teen bragged about the vacations he took with his white friends, as well as about his ability to "talk white."

Conversations in Groveland revealed a preference for goods and services provided by and for whites. For example, the planning committee for the St. Catherine's reunion decided early on to hire a black-owned catering service, but in the end, Etta, one of the organizers, changed the plan:

> We're just going to get some trays from [a large grocery store chain]. I'm going to the one by my job on the North Shore [Chicago's overwhelmingly white lakefront suburbs]. Those ones up there are the best. And I hear that whatever they do, they do really nice things. Up there, you just snap your fingers and they're ready for you. They do things quick.

Like African Americans' evaluations of white businesses, perceptions of white neighborhoods were often positive. According to Mr. Charles:

> If you look at Weston [a white community], for instance, you will find that they have banks and businesses in their community and that they support those banks and businesses. We [African Americans] have to begin to buy from our own. But we just cannot buy from ours because we are black. We have to understand that it helps the community. It provides jobs. It is rein-

vested in the banks in our community. [Black] businesses have to forget about being better than the people
they sell to. They have to become consumer conscious.
They have to be sensitive to what the people want. I am
talking about an attitude change. Look at those stable
white communities—they have what the black communities have been missing.[11]

Local youths also viewed some white institutions posi-
tively. Chicago has an extensive community college system,
and Kesha Tims, a youth-group member, attended Johnson
College in a predominantly white neighborhood on the
Southwest Side. Another community college is much closer
to Groveland, but Kesha justified her choice, noting, "Johnson is a little better. You know, where the white people are."
According to youth-group member Leslie Wilson, nearby
Boylston Community College was "just like the ghetto."
Blacks accounted for less than 1 percent of the community
surrounding Johnson (which is adjacent to Beltway) in 1990,
while the area surrounding Boylston College—the southeast-
ern corridor into which the Black Belt has expanded—was
98 percent black.

Another African American youngster, thirteen-year-old
Mary Compton, reflected on her decision to attend a high
school known for its diverse population rather than the
mostly black local high school: "I figure, I been to all-black
school for nine years and I ain't got no problem with
myself . . . But, I figure, when I start looking at colleges and

then after college, it's going to be a lot of different kinds of people, so I might as well go to a school like that."

Why did the residents of Groveland display a more congenial racial attitude and greater racial tolerance than those of Beltway, Dover, and Archer Park? There are several reasons. For one thing, Groveland residents were firmly in control of neighborhood institutions. They did not face an influx of other ethnic groups, so they were not competing for housing and public space. Whites, Latinos, and Asians tended to shy away from African American neighborhoods, even those that are middle class. For example, the rapid growth of Chicago's Latino population was not reflected in the demographic composition of black neighborhoods.

Equally important, unlike upper-middle-class African American professionals—for whom competition with whites and other groups for coveted positions in private companies and universities had become an obsession— black adults in Groveland faced less racial competition for desirable jobs.[12] Many residents held civil-service and unionized jobs such as teacher, bus driver, city infrastructure worker, and park district employee, and federal positions in the post office and Social Security Administration.

In fact, in 2000, 27 percent of the employed population in Groveland worked for the city, state, or federal government. That figure was almost five times the proportion of Archer Park residents, four times the proportion of Dover residents, and six percentage points higher than the proportion in Beltway.[13] In civil-service jobs, especially those obtained through formal tests, racially motivated decisions were much less likely to determine hiring, salary increases, and promotions. Thus Groveland adults were less likely to feel the slings and arrows of racial slights in workplace settings, or to encounter "glass ceilings"—invisible but impenetrable barriers to better job assignments.

Finally, outside the sphere of employment, Groveland residents tended to spend less of their lives in predominantly white society. They did not live in largely white neighborhoods, as do many upwardly mobile black professionals, and they rarely engaged whites and other ethnic groups in social settings such as cocktail parties, school events, and public playgrounds. Accordingly, they experienced fewer painful and cumulative racial indignities and less outright prejudice.

Of course, even though racial antagonisms and tensions were relatively weak in Groveland, residents did reveal some mistrust of white institutions. For example, one Groveland teenager at an elite, racially integrated Catholic school outside the neighborhood expressed frustration with the day's discussion of affirmative action and the gulf between his views and those of his white classmates. Similarly, a retired black construction worker recalled his days laboring among whites, when his work was always scrutinized for flaws and his skills went underutilized. And Groveland chose not to join the Southeast Side Home-Equity Program, which was designed to reduce housing turnover by providing incentives to homeowners to remain in the community. Community Council member Bill Mason noted that FOR SALE signs were acceptable in black communities, in contrast to white communities, which considered them "an invitation to blacks . . . In white neighborhoods, the only way that you will see the property is if the Realtor shows you."[14]

At the Fisherman's Catch restaurant, an older black patron commented on the scene: "Back thirty years all this used to be white." When surveying today's business landscape, he contrasted what he viewed as the dismally performing African American stores with the prospering Asian American–owned shops. "They got all that merchandise and they can get money from the bank for that stuff. Black man try to go in the bank for a loan and they want to see your track record—what you been doin.' The government help out those Koreans to get them stores."

Residents agreed that racial discrimination not only existed in Groveland's past but also continued to live on as a daily reality in the broader society, including in schools and workplaces. As resident Felton Anders told a church youth group in explaining why he was denied promotions at work, "Racism is still alive." Residents reported harassment by white police officers, racial slurs cast in their direction, and repeated mispronunciation of their names. Experiences with the open and brutal discrimination perpetrated against blacks during the 1960s, and the harsh Jim Crow segregation experienced by the large number of northern blacks with southern roots, fostered widespread agreement with claims of invisible racism.

This consensus boosted the likelihood that residents would accept hazy descriptions of racial incidents as fact. For example, Willie invoked discrimination to explain why a train passed through Groveland one morning without stopping, causing him to be late for work: "What I wanna know is why it's gon' stop at [Benton Heights] and don't stop at [Groveland]?" Although Willie could not see the train stop at Benton Heights, he knew that it was the only integrated neighborhood in southeast Chicago, and that residents of Benton Heights were mainly upper-middle-class professionals, whereas Groveland was black and lower-middle-class. No bottles were thrown or racial slurs cast, yet Willie's awareness of pervasive racial bias led him to invoke discrimination as the probable cause of the incident.

Even the younger generation, who grew up in Groveland after whites had fled, often saw discrimination where it may not necessarily have existed. For example, seventeen-year-old Robert Morgan attended St. Gregory High School, a competitive, integrated Catholic institution outside the neighborhood. In his senior year he tried unsuccessfully to switch from his mainstream English class into Honors English. This was the topic of discussion one evening at an informal rap session with his friends at St. Catherine's youth group. Robert reported that he had enrolled in an English class called Melting Pot. He wanted to take it for Honors because he was getting an A in the class, but his previous English teacher had not recommended him for Honors. A girl in an apparently similar situation had successfully switched to Honors, prompting Robert to meet with his counselor to see if he could do the same. However, the counselor told him that nothing could be done without the sponsorship of his previous English teacher.

Robert grew irritated by what he perceived as different treatment of similar requests. Trae, one of the youth-group members, commented, "That dark skin didn't help you." (He was talking about Robert's race, not his particular skin tone.) As Robert continued to complain, Trae asked of the girl, "What race was she?" Robert replied, "Irish." Lawrence, another youth-group member, said, "Now you get it?" Trae further remarked, "Whites get special treatment, and even the Hispanics get treated good, too. It's only the black students that don't get the breaks." The facts of the case may not be as clear as Trae and Lawrence assumed, but the participants in this all-black setting accepted race as the deciding factor.

To the outside observer, some of the interracial experiences in Groveland seemed petty, even humorous. For example, the local school council chastised a representative from a publishing company whose sample yearbooks featured only white students. The council—only half-seriously—pressed the representative: Why did she think that her company was qualified to produce a yearbook for a predominantly black school if it had no samples of what such a yearbook might look like?

Incidents such as these—filed as acts of discrimination—fueled the use of racial frames in other situations. General distrust of white intentions and predominantly white institutions is an important aspect of the racial attitudes of blacks,[15] and the cycle of discrimination appeared inexorable to Groveland residents. Still, such negative sentiments did not dominate discussions among the neighborhood's inhabitants.

Groveland's racial homogeneity allowed residents to engage instead in the daily work of defining a black community. African Americans pursued this task by recognizing differences in mannerisms, beliefs, styles, and practices between blacks and nonblacks, particularly whites. Residents relied on these characterizations to articulate whom they included within racial boundaries, and to censor those who engaged in behavior or aligned themselves with issues associated with nonblacks.

DEFINING RACIAL BOUNDARIES

"My stepmother was very [into the] 'society' thing," remarked Carla May, a twenty-five-year-old Groveland resident, remembering her childhood. "She would bring us up ... like ... how white people bring up they kids—ballet, tap, ice skating, clarinet, piano—I mean, you know." Because of her stepmother's insistence on raising her "how white people bring up they kids," Carla eventually left and moved in with her grandmother, preferring to ride her bike and engage in other forms of recreation or amusement with her black friends.

Carla rebelled against participating in "white activities" and saw no value in conforming to a set of social mores that she associated with white culture. Her actions helped mark a racial boundary—a process that has both positive and negative implications.[16] While it serves to solidify a black identity, it may hinder racial integration when people refuse to play the game according to the rules of the majority culture.[17]

Efforts to maintain racial boundaries often take the form of stereotypical characterizations of nonblacks that set forth an idea of the "other." For example, St. Catherine's school held its alumni reunion during the Thanksgiving holiday. A small number of white alumni attended the event, which was planned primarily by younger black alumni. One of the organizers asked a volunteer who was working at the door if everything was going smoothly. The volunteer answered that it was, other than the fact that the room was much too cold. The alumnus answered, "Yeah, we told Father [John] to turn on the heat, but you know how they are. They like that cold. Look [*gesturing toward two white alumni*]—they don't even feel it." These remarks delineated the perceived line between black and white: whites like the cold, blacks do not.

This subtle racial undercurrent pervaded other venues as well. The youth group at St. Catherine jokingly complained that Father John and Sister Tina, both white, clapped off the beat when directing the choir. Furthermore, when asked about the girls' basketball team at a predominantly white high school, one youth-group member replied, "They pretty good—for some white girls."

Participants in such discussions tacitly understand that not everyone will fulfill *all* stereotypes: some black choir members clap off the beat, and some white basketball players, such as Larry Bird, have risen to the top in the National Basketball Association. Still, these allowances do not debunk the entire mythical structure sustained through social conversation and the popular media, especially movies. Ron Shelton's *White Men Can't Jump*—a 1992 movie pairing the

African American Wesley Snipes with the white Woody Harrelson as basketball-playing con artists—abounds with remarks specifying the socially accepted places for whites and blacks, especially in neighborhood sports.

More serious attempts to modify behavior by invoking racial boundaries also occurred. In climbing the socioeconomic ladder, for example, some Groveland residents had mastered both black and white communication styles. However, other residents continued to challenge their neighbors' involvement with whites. Willie, a resident of Groveland in his thirties, lived in both black and white worlds. He grew up in the neighborhood, ran with the local gang, went to public high school, and took classes at a nearby community college. In the afternoon Willie worked as a recreation counselor in Groveland, but in the morning he worked as a runner at the Mercantile Exchange in downtown Chicago.[18] When he returned to the neighborhood he had to switch from talking to white coworkers to interacting with black neighborhood friends, and he always had a story to tell about his job. One of these stories illustrates his ability to communicate in both places:

> I be on the phone downtown. Down at the Merc. I was talkin' to this white lady on the phone. You know I was the only black guy workin' for this company. One time we had to meet this lady, and she was lookin' me dead in my face. She looked like she seen a ghost. I was like, "Is there a problem?" She couldn't believe I was black. I had people down there tellin' me I sound Italian . . .

After Willie related another story about the Merc, Keith, a longtime friend of his from the neighborhood, challenged in a friendly manner his association with whites. Addressing Willie as a member of the Raps gang, with which they were both associated, he prodded, "Raps, you like them muthafuckas, don't you? You always talkin' about 'em. You like the muthafuckas?" Willie answered in a facetiously proper voice, "Some of my best friends are white, Keith." Keith asked another question, "Raps, you be, um, you be changin' yo' um, um, speech when you be down there?" Willie replied, "Naw, but I gotta talk clear when I'm on the phone." To this, another friend, Scott, joked that Willie's employers gave him a shot in the arm every day so he would turn white while he was at work.

This interaction illustrates a number of efforts to negotiate boundaries. Willie crossed boundaries by using standard English at the office and black English at the park. While he clearly was comfortable with both sets of mannerisms, he recognized that each had its place, and lamented that members of the younger black generation would have trouble finding jobs because of their inability to communicate effectively using standard English. Of course, the African American community in Groveland included blacks who spoke standard English, took clarinet lessons, and associated with whites regularly. Still, attempts to push beyond the boundaries the community had established through language and culture often led to immediate correction.

Other telling examples reveal how Groveland residents police racial boundaries. In aldermanic races throughout the

1990s, much controversy surrounded the relative "blackness" of the candidates. One race pitted Trisha Hill—the incumbent and a close ally of the city's Democratic leadership—against Rick Dumbar, a formidable challenger. Dumbar attacked Hill's connection with the white mayor, Richard Daley, warning that the white Democratic machine would certainly reappear if voters supported Daley and his nonwhite allies, such as Hill.

Redistricting was the election's chief issue: Dumbar and a number of black incumbents believed that the city council should include more African Americans. Remapping the city to create more predominantly black wards lay at the heart of their strategy. Dumbar's campaign literature asserted that "there are presently 19 black wards in this city and it should be 3 more, which would give the black community 22 wards." The same flyer also attacked Hill's stance, noting "Alderman Hill and boss Daley do not want this . . . Don't be fooled!!! Don't be tricked!!!" Connecting Hill with "boss Daley" was a particularly piercing strategy, as the term resonated with both corrupt politics and racist paternalism.

The Hill campaign naturally protested this characterization, and Hill supporters, sensitive to Dumbar's claims, asked her to clarify her position on the remapping issue. Hill provided a lengthy reply on the subject she considered the "most complicated and important" of the campaign:

Every ten years the government does the census, and about a year later the numbers are certified and sent to municipalities. The 1990 census said there was a loss of population in the traditionally African American communities . . . A group of African American aldermen got together to work with the Urban League to talk about ways to ensure greater African American participation in the city government through possible remapping of city wards. During these talks, there was a lot of conversation about coming together for a united agenda. But the remapping configuration did a lot of things to the ward [which encompasses Groveland] . . . The resulting population would be about 60 percent black and 40 percent Hispanic and ethnic white. According to the Voting Rights Act, they should try to keep "communities of interest" together, and this plan does not do that.

Numerous individuals grumbled at community meetings and in informal conversations that Hill was a "sellout" because she opposed a large group of African American politicians, and her supporters urged her to speak much more forcefully about her commitment to the black community. Her campaign responded by highlighting the number of African Americans promoted under the ward's current leadership, and by pointing out Hill's assistance to African American businesses. Hill also responded by tempering her references to Mayor Daley, who was running for reelection against a black candidate, asserting, "People are going to vote for who they want to for mayor, whether it may be Joe Gardner or Daley. The bottom line is their [community] services, and they look to their alderman for that." At another meeting, she commented, "And yes, I work closely with the present mayor of Chicago. But I will work closely with whoever is elected mayor. Because if there is a person you can't dialogue with, you can't ask for—demand anything for—your community."

With the strength of a thirty-year-old political organization and the clout of three elected state and city officials in her corner, Hill won 65 percent of the vote. Still, Dumbar's campaign reminded Hill that straying too far beyond the bounds of acceptable behavior could be dangerous, and Hill's swift and measured responses revealed the seriousness of such charges. While some writers depict African Americans as holding a singular position in attempting to define a sense of community, experiences in Groveland suggest a more complicated picture.[19] When Hill's political rivals attempted to characterize her activities as violating racial boundaries, her campaign responded with equally fervent attempts to persuade citizens to support her more flexible definitions of those boundaries.

Individual residents must balance their personal proclivities and aspirations against the expectations shared and reinforced by the community, and in so doing they constantly question the definition of blackness. Like Willie, some residents pursued interactions that perched precariously on the border, yet they managed to skillfully adapt to their environments, thereby helping to sustain and expand existing borders.

PRESERVING THE NEIGHBORHOOD
BY MARKING CLASS DISTINCTIONS

While broad limits on appropriate black and white behavior help solidify residents' identity as African Americans, those limits also help residents distinguish their positions *within* black society. Groveland represents a specific social niche within the African American community, and residents spent considerable time differentiating themselves from other groups of blacks.

The diminished role of race in the neighborhood's social organization did not reflect a lack of anxiety about community change. In fact, residents expressed serious concern about the pressures of living in an area surrounded by ghetto neighborhoods. Because their community could undergo a class transformation, residents closely scrutinized newcomers. Newer residents often challenged traditions established by older residents, boosting anxiety about the neighborhood's future. Commenting on these residents, Mariane Johnson remarked:

> In fact, over the next five to eight years . . . that's going to be the time the houses are going to be available . . . And that's when things are going to begin to turn. They're turning now, but there's going to be a real influx of people. I'm not sure [in what direction] because you know I haven't been too impressed. You know, just on this street, we've had a couple people

move in and they're not, you know, they don't understand about block clubs, you know. The block, you
know, we have people they trying to work on they cars
on the street. And this may sound really trivial, but if
you don't maintain your standards . . . We have garages
and alleys, that's where you do that stuff, back there,
okay.

Gradual in-migration of families from nearby low-income
neighborhoods had already made Groveland slightly more
economically diverse. The community's unemployment rate
rose from 4 to 12 percent from 1970 to 1990, and the proportion of families with incomes below the poverty line grew
from 5 to 12 percent. Although both unemployment and
poverty dipped during the economic boom period of the latter 1990s, by 2000 they were still significantly higher than in
1970.[20] Groveland's 8 percent poverty rate in 2000 remained
below that of the city as a whole (10 percent), and well below
the 18 percent rate for Chicago's black residents.[21] However,
long-standing residents were well aware that the rising number of lower-income residents could herald a sustained decline in the neighborhood's socioeconomic profile.

Residents did not discuss these changes in terms of
poverty statistics. Rather, they talked about the increase in
gang membership, growing numbers of out-of-wedlock preg-
nancies, drug houses, renters (including families receiving
federal Section 8 housing subsidies), and residents who failed
to maintain their homes and lawns.[22] During our research, a

major South Side gang was using the park's field house as its headquarters.[23] Residents sensed the fragility of their neighborhood, and block-club members talked constantly about problems arising from the neighborhood's proximity to high-crime areas, and how to address them.

Adolescents in a middle-class community that abuts inner-city ghettos are more likely to be influenced by habits, styles, and outlooks associated with such areas than are their counterparts in communities far removed from such influences. Several youngsters not involved with gangs carried guns when not in school, for example, and one left a gun lying near a basketball court. These youths viewed toting a pistol as a sign of status as well as style, like wearing the latest Nike shoes.[24] Although there was no indication that any of these guns had been fired, the threat of violence was always present. On one occasion, after some youths had argued on a neighborhood basketball court, one ran home to get his gun. Fortunately, his target had disappeared by the time the youth reappeared.

The visible presence of firearms in the neighborhood raised sobering concerns about crime, and apprehension about violent crime became pervasive. An older man in a church choir walked women to and from their cars before and after rehearsals because of these concerns. And, as noted previously, those planning a high school class reunion were concerned for the safety of white alumni as they walked from the parking lot to the reunion or stepped outside the event to smoke.

Aware of burglaries and other crimes associated with drug dealing, Groveland residents worked hard to keep crime under control. In fact, they believed their community did quite well in preventing crime, and did not have a serious problem compared with other black neighborhoods. Nonetheless, Groveland residents were much more likely to be exposed to crime and other manifestations of social disarray because of their location on the South Side—an area with relatively high crime rates—than were similar middle-class communities elsewhere. For example, residents sometimes reported hearing gunshots at night. Thus, given the absence of in-migration of other racial and ethnic groups, residents discussed threats to their way of life in terms of class, not race.

CLASS CHANGES AND THE FUTURE
OF GROVELAND

The lower-middle-class black community of Groveland openly negotiated what it means to be African American in today's society. The heritage photographs, African American music, seasonal decorations, landscaped gardens, and block-club signs underscored the neighborhood's black ownership and middle-class standards. Despite the precarious nature of identity, residents perceived themselves as both separate and modest, as demonstrated by Willie's ability to negotiate black and white settings and by the community's aversion to "bourgie" lifestyles. The suspicion—difficult to substantiate but equally difficult to eliminate—persisted that racism limits the opportunities of blacks, yet Groveland residents focused primarily on the changing nature of their own identity rather than on contesting the power of the external white majority. Residents constantly pushed boundaries and interpreted racial interactions as they defined black identity as resisting or opposed to white identity.

However, concerns about black identity did not cause Groveland residents to obscure the significance of class distinctions within the black community. As noted above, whereas the neighborhoods of Beltway and Dover struggled with the challenges of ethnic change, the residents of Groveland confronted the challenges of class changes within their neighborhood. And, like Beltway, they reacted to these challenges by systematically attempting to address them rather than by exiting to other neighborhoods. Using Albert Hirschman's language, voice trumped exit in confronting the threat of neighborhood change in Groveland.

The use of the voice option was aided by a sense of loyalty to the community. Indeed, if loyalty to a neighborhood is measured in terms of the low rate of housing turnover—that is, the extent to which people reside in the same residence for an extended period of time—Groveland residents were the most loyal (see Table 1, Appendix B). This loyalty is perhaps a reason why few chose the exit option when confronted with the constant threat of an invasion of lower-income blacks from adjacent ghetto neighborhoods.

Instead of exiting the neighborhood, the residents largely resorted to voice by working vigorously to maintain neighborhood stability through active block clubs, the most symbolic feature of the social organization of the neighborhood. In sharp contrast to the transient population of Archer Park, Groveland residents dedicated themselves to constructing enduring institutions, especially schools and churches, and the neighborhood supported an active business district and a clean and safe public park.

Just as Beltwayites used the option of voice in complex ways to preserve the ethnic makeup of their neighborhood, so, too, did the residents of Groveland in their efforts to preserve the class makeup of theirs. The residents of both Beltway and Groveland were aware of the strength and effectiveness of their respective neighborhood social organizations in resisting undesirable changes. This reduced the likelihood that the residents would react to the possibility of unwanted changes by leaving the neighborhood.

CHAPTER SIX

Neighborhood Racial Conflict and Social Policy Dilemmas

A merica has often been characterized as a melting pot, constantly creating an ever-changing blend of races and cultures. Indeed, many citizens still cling to the notion that the residential desegregation of neighborhoods is achievable.[1] The research conducted for this book, however, strongly suggests that neighborhoods in urban America, especially in large metropolitan areas like Chicago, are likely to remain divided, racially and culturally. This has profound implications for the future of race and ethnic relations in the United States; national racial tensions cannot be disassociated from tensions originating in neighborhood social dynamics.

Persistent racial and ethnic divisions in neighborhoods come from the tendency to make distinctions between people in terms of ancestry, systems of shared communication, cultural preferences, and physical and social environments. Over time, and given the degree of intergroup contact, these distinctions become associated with differences in traditions, belief systems, values, worldviews, linguistic patterns, even skills. Imposed or voluntary restrictions on actions may enhance these differences and in turn diminish opportunities for economic and social advancement. Under such situations, "social factors such as level of economic well-being interact with cultural factors in the formation of observed group traits and characteristics."[2]

The more individuals within groups perceive and highlight these differences, the less likely they are to welcome others or to feel comfortable sharing the same physical and social spaces. In some situations, groups voluntarily separate after contact is established, particularly when one group enjoys superior resources and can see no benefit, or possibly even detriment, from being associated with the out-group, whether that association involves social interaction or merely sharing physical space. In other situations, separation is imposed, and its existence reflects a power struggle between dominant and subordinate groups: the former is able to successfully restrict the movement of the latter through forms of residential, educational, and occupational discrimination, often justified by racist ideologies.

The more entrenched the system of racial stratification, the less likely it is that challenges to established racial arrangements will even arise, much less be successful. In America, such challenges have increasingly occurred as the system of racial stratification has weakened over the years in the face of growing urbanization and industrialization. Industrial expansion and the concomitant decline of rural life throughout the twentieth century drew minority groups to urban areas. There they could enjoy the benefits of working in the wage economy and accumulate the resources that promote social advancement in society.

Cities afford greater educational and occupational opportunities than do rural or agricultural areas. The usual political, social, and economic imperatives of urban living have long provided greater opportunities to develop viable minority institutions such as schools, churches, political and labor organizations, and professional and business associations. The high concentration of minority individuals in urban neighborhoods facilitates communication, promotes ideological development, secures group identity, and enhances collective action. For all these reasons, urban minority groups are in a far better position to mount an offensive against racial oppression and to move into more fluid or less restrictive patterns of intergroup interaction.[3] The growing development and subsequent mobilization of political pressure by the urban black population, for example, pushed state and federal government agencies to mediate and resolve racial conflicts, including the interventions that eroded Jim Crow segregation.

However, black political pressure could not forestall the growth of de facto segregation when African Americans moved to cities. Population pressures due to the increased migration of African Americans to the city of Chicago led to an expansion of segregated ghetto neighborhoods, as blacks eventually spilled over into adjacent areas that whites were vacating. In the 1970s, whites fled ethnic working-class neighborhoods on the South Side in substantial numbers. Although most migrated to the suburbs, some—especially those tied to city employment—relocated to predominantly white working-class neighborhoods in the northwest and southwest parts of the city, neighborhoods like Beltway and Dover.

During the last two decades of the twentieth century, however, the rapid growth of Chicago's Latino population provided an added dimension to neighborhood ethnic conflict. Latino entry into neighborhoods on the Southwest Side of Chicago further spurred white flight to other neighborhoods in the city and to the suburbs. Moreover, the rapid growth in the Latino population increased the potential for Latino-black frictions, especially when the two groups competed for scarce public resources in the larger city or in areas within or near their respective neighborhoods. This study shows that in a city experiencing ongoing ethnic migration, the metamorphosis of neighborhoods continues and expressions of ethnic antagonisms vary in subtle ways.

But intergroup antagonisms in urban neighborhoods are not limited to issues of race and ethnicity. Social-class antagonisms are also present—not only those inextricably linked to racial antagonisms, as when negative feelings held by whites toward poor blacks reflect a combination of race and class hostilities, but also those that represent intragroup hostilities, as when middle-class blacks make disparaging comments about poor blacks. It would be a serious mistake to view racial or ethnic groups as monolithic social and economic entities.

Members of individual ethnic and racial groups vary along social and economic lines, and this is reflected in terms of experiences, human-capital traits (such as years of schooling, specialized training, etc.), degree of contact with other ethnic and racial groups, and so on. This is particularly true in a society where the life chances of people of color depend as much on economic class position as they do on race.[4] Reactions to behavior attributed to class differences are often similar to reactions attributed to race and ethnic differences.

The essential point is that long-standing or current residents often see the presence, even the threat, of different ethnic, racial, and class groups in neighborhoods as undesirable. In Beltway and Dover, citizens' concerns were mainly about racial and ethnic presence. Anxiety over blacks and the increased entrance of Latinos into the neighborhood consumed Beltway's white population. When Dover was largely white, the residents also worried about black and Latino penetration. But after Dover became a Latino enclave, the major shared concern was keeping African Americans at bay.

Archer Park and Groveland were both, at one time, predominantly white, and flight was the response to the influx of Latinos and blacks, respectively, into those neighborhoods. Since the ethnic makeup of both neighborhoods had been firmly established, concerns about group penetration mainly reflected issues of social class. Many Archer Park residents viewed the increasing overcrowding caused by the continuous migration of poor Mexicans as less than desirable, and African Americans in Groveland were anxious about the gradual appearance of poor blacks from surrounding neighborhoods.

In a comparative sense there were some marked and subtle differences in group responses to the changing neighborhood dynamics in these four communities that reflect varying levels of intergroup tensions. Nonetheless, the behavioral responses we observed in our fieldwork are quite consistent with Albert Hirschman's theory of exit, voice, and loyalty.[5]

THE CHANGING FACE
OF URBAN ETHNIC NEIGHBORHOODS

Beltway. Faced with the options of both exit and voice, residents in Beltway have, for the most part, resisted the former alternative. Many had already exited neighborhoods on the South Side of Chicago in response to the growing presence of African Americans. Although high rates of residential stability and racial and class homogeneity have, over the years, provided a solid foundation for neighborhood social organization and the maintenance of social control, residents nonetheless worried about the future of their community. Our discussions with Beltwayites revealed that the possible arrival of significant numbers of African Americans, Latinos, and Asians was viewed as a threat to the neighborhood's way of life. Residents saw other neighborhoods change from white-ethnic strongholds to minority enclaves, and those transformations were often accompanied by rising rates of crime, declining property values, and the erosion of neighborhood social institutions.

As has already been mentioned, the exit possibility does not depend solely on an actual threat; it may also be based on a perceived or potential threat. The frequently held view was that the neighborhood could be in danger if certain developments were to materialize. Aware that their neighborhood, like many other formerly white enclaves, could be transformed into a haven for minorities, Beltway residents saw their neighborhood as "the last garden spot in Chicago"; that is, the last of the stable, white, working-class neighborhoods. "Beltway is the last stand" was a popular slogan. It revealed that voice was favored over exit. There are two main reasons for this.

The more obvious reason is that a good percentage of the employed adults in Beltway were on the city's payroll.[6] Their employment status required them to live within the city of Chicago. Thus, leaving their neighborhood was not a viable option. Indeed, in terms of neighborhood stability and social amenities, there were no affordable white working-class areas in the city that constituted a better alternative to Beltway. But voice also took precedence over exit because Beltwayites were fully aware that the neighborhood's strong foundation for stability provided a more than reasonable chance to prevent an ethnic turnover.

Accordingly, there was intense community pressure to maintain a high level of social organization: residents reminded one another to work vigilantly to keep the neighborhood strong and thereby reduce the threat of advancement by outside groups. The prevailing view was that if the neighborhood were allowed to deteriorate, some residents would be encouraged to leave; African Americans and Latinos from nearby communities could then fill the resulting vacancies. Residents were called upon to keep yards clean, to curb gangs, to supervise their children, to remove graffiti, and to work actively to attract new businesses.

Beltway's ability to achieve and sustain a relatively high

level of social organization over the years could be attributed to several factors, including residential stability, racial and class homogeneity, a network of dense acquaintanceships, extended families, vibrant community institutions, and powerful connections to the city's political structure. Consequently, the common goal of maintaining stability in the ethnic and racial makeup of the neighborhood was more easily achieved.

A strong common belief system also contributed to the social organization of Beltway. Integrating sentiments concerning the adherence to neighborhood standards with patriotism and social conservatism, this belief system helped to generate a sense of what Hirschman calls loyalty. In fact, our field-workers found that expressions of loyalty were not uncommon in Beltway. As one married woman emphatically put it, "We're raising our kids here, and I don't know about you, but we ain't going nowhere." If loyalty reinforces voice and discourages exit, Beltway has benefited from the attachment of many residents to the neighborhood.

Nonetheless, despite the expressions of loyalty and vigorous efforts to keep the neighborhood stable, during the 1990s the white population of Beltway decreased (13.5 percent), while the number of minority residents increased, especially Latinos (from 7.5 percent to 21 percent). Our research was conducted in Beltway during the first half of the 1990s, and the residents were fully aware of the demographic changes in the neighborhood, especially the rise in the number of Latino homeowners. However, as Hubert Blalock has pointed out, white residents in neighborhoods with an influx of outside groups and who find it too expensive or too difficult to retreat to areas where few or no nonwhites reside will likely remain.[7] Thus, given the significant presence of municipal workers required to live within the city's boundaries, combined with Beltway's relatively high level of social organization, voice may continue to trump exit in the short run, if not over the long haul.

Dover. In sharp contrast to Beltway's relative stability stands the large exit of whites from Dover. Once an area of working-class Eastern European immigrants, Dover has become a Mexican American enclave. Since 1990 whites have overwhelmingly chosen the exit option and are now represented by only 19 percent of the population. Before the arrival of Mexican Americans in large numbers, Dover was struggling through economic decline. Industrial layoffs combined with the out-migration of many who had acquired the means to buy homes in the suburbs created housing vacancies and lowered property values. Beginning in the 1980s the en masse in-migration of Latinos, many from adjacent Mexican American enclaves, counteracted this trend by sharply increasing housing demand and population density.

Rapid social change influences institutional arrangements and patterns of behavior. The Mexican arrivals were younger than the white residents who remained, and language and cultural differences further separated the groups. Tensions between whites and Latinos simmered beneath the surface and were occasionally vented in public situations, most frequently in conflicts over language use.

During the period of our research, white business and civic organizations were in decline mainly due to a reluctance or an inability to attract Latino participants to fill vacancies created by an aging or fleeing white population. Local churches, on the other hand, drew large numbers of Latino residents, but cultural clashes resulted in ethnic divisions, and the two groups tended to segregate themselves. These developments were indicative of weak neighborhood social organization that encouraged whites to exit the neighborhood in increasing numbers throughout the 1990s. However, whites and Latinos in Dover did find common ground in their response to African Americans. Latinos in Dover—even the recent migrants—were no more open to living with black Americans than were the white residents. Anti-black sentiment was fueled by concerns over Dover's close proximity to black ghetto neighborhoods that featured high rates of joblessness and the problems that accompany an acute lack of employment. Although Latino enclaves provided a buffer between Dover and the poor African American neighborhoods, it was a thin cushion at best.

Given the neighborhood's proximity to poor black areas, efforts to prevent African Americans from residing in Dover and the busing of students from overcrowded Dover schools to adjacent poor black neighborhoods presented a rare opportunity for wide-scale white-Latino cooperation. Schools, then, provided a setting for ethnic integration and cooperation as Mexican and white parents joined forces to pressure officials to build more classrooms in Dover and thus eliminate the practice of busing.

In the final analysis, the rapid exodus of whites from Dover will very likely continue. What distinguished whites in Dover from whites in Beltway was that prejudiced remarks in Beltway accompanied feelings that they had to prepare to confront an impending threat, whereas prejudiced comments among whites in Dover were associated with feelings that they had "lost the battle." Aside from the cross-ethnic efforts of Dover parents to combat school overcrowding, the exit option has overwhelmed the potential for whites' use of voice—that is, taking steps to correct or address what they perceive to be undesirable changes in the neighborhood. And despite the substantial decline in the number of white residents during the 1990s, the total population of Dover increased from 32,000 to 45,000 during the same period, due to the growth of Latino residents.

Indeed, given the overall increase of the Latino population in Chicago, Latino families that leave Dover for other communities will be replaced by other Latino families moving in. For all these reasons Dover will remain a Latino enclave for the foreseeable future. Given the burgeoning Latino population's demand for housing, issues of loyalty, which were so crucial in maintaining the dominant white population in Beltway, were not as important for preserving the Mexican makeup of Dover.

Archer Park. Issues of loyalty are even less important for preserving the ethnic makeup of Archer Park. In the latter decades of the twentieth century, Archer Park changed from a neighborhood overwhelmingly populated by whites, many of them of Bohemian heritage, to a stronghold for Mexican Americans. Indeed, Mexican Americans have been the dominant population in Archer Park since the 1970s. And unlike in Dover and Beltway, residents expressed little concern about neighborhood ethnic change or ethnic or racial challenges to their prerogatives. Except for a few immobile elderly residents, whites have very nearly vanished from the neighborhood. Although our study found that the African American population had increased on the outer fringes of Archer Park, and although a continuous stream of upwardly mobile Latino residents were exiting Archer Park, these trends were counterbalanced by the steady flow of foreign-born Mexicans into the neighborhood. Mexicans were, therefore, firmly in control of the neighborhood and its major institutions, including schools.

Yet it was not a neighborhood that held even the Mexican residents. Upwardly mobile Mexicans exited as soon as they acquired sufficient financial resources to do so. Of our four neighborhoods, Archer Park most clearly distinguished itself as a "stepping-stone" community. Many of the upwardly mobile residents moved to the suburbs or to higher-status Chicago communities, such as Dover, at the first opportunity. Indeed, Dover, which ranked above Archer Park in terms of housing prices and class status, included many Mexican residents who once lived in Archer Park.

Signs of transience rather than permanence pervaded Archer Park; during our time there, even longtime residents expressed a feeling of longing for another neighborhood. This lack of attachment or loyalty to the neighborhood reduced the use of the voice option. Conditions in the neighborhood were less than desirable due in large measure to the extreme overcrowding created by the steady and heavy stream of immigrants from Mexico, as well as by the in-migration of residents from the nearby Mexican community of Pilsen. Yet residents invested little effort in the social organization of the neighborhood with the hope of improving the quality of life. In other words, there was little collective supervision of community activities, and little participation in voluntary organizations such as block clubs, civic and business clubs, parent-teacher organizations, and political groups. The residents simply left Archer Park as soon as they got the chance.

Accordingly, the lack of a perceived threat to Mexican dominance in Archer Park and the low commitment to the neighborhood as a permanent place of residence decreased concerns among residents about the future of the neighborhood and its institutions. Indeed, issues of race and ethnicity were not reflected in the social organization of Archer Park. Yet ethnic antagonisms did prevail. The few remaining elderly whites, although resigned to the idea that Archer Park had become a Mexican enclave, evinced bitterness about the ethnic and cultural changes in the neighborhood and exhibited hostility toward their Mexican neighbors. Moreover, competition among Latinos, blacks, and elderly whites for the use of facilities at the parks and playgrounds contributed to ethnic tensions. Finally, and most fundamentally, Mexican animus toward African Americans in Archer Park revolved around attempts to differentiate themselves from blacks in terms of symbols of social prestige in the larger society.

The more loyal or attached residents are to a neighborhood, the greater the degree of ethnic tensions when the neighborhood is threatened with the possibility of an ethnic turnover. Not only was Archer Park free of any threat of ethnic transformation, but our research suggested that there was relatively little loyalty among the residents in the neighborhood. Accordingly, unlike in Beltway and in Dover, where hostility toward blacks had been associated with concerns about neighborhood ethnic preservation or control of institutions such as local schools, expressions of racial antagonism among Archer Park Latinos derived mainly from their efforts to differentiate themselves from African Americans and thereby ensure that they avoided the stigmas associated with race.

Groveland. If residential stability is a sign of loyalty to a neighborhood, the residents of Groveland were perhaps the most loyal of our four communities. Relatively few families exited the neighborhood once they arrived. The residential turnover, measured in terms of those living in the same house over a five-year period, was the lowest among the four neighborhoods in this study.[8] Moreover, in contrast to the palpable racial and ethnic antagonisms in Beltway and Dover and the evident, if not as intense, animosities in Archer Park, ethnic and racial antagonisms in the African American neighborhood of Groveland were far less obvious.

Nonetheless, this lower-middle-class black neighborhood continually struggled with the issues associated with being African American in contemporary U.S. society. Race remained a topic of discussion even though interracial contact within Groveland was minimal. However, although the racial dialogue in Groveland included some anti-white sentiments, it did not reverberate with the hostile expressions about other groups so typically seen in statements made by Dover, Beltway, and Archer Park residents. In fact, discussions about race observed by our field researchers overwhelmingly reflected concerns about forging a positive black identity rather than overtly contesting the dominant white population.

Several factors accounted for the relatively neutral racial attitudes in Groveland. A substantial number of the neighborhood's lower-middle-class blacks worked in government jobs,[9] whose rules of hiring and employment restricted competition that might be attributed solely to racial reasons. The employment conditions of many Groveland residents reduced concerns that consume upper-middle-class black professionals in the larger society, where the more subjective nature of employment leads to anxieties about racial bias in salary differentials and promotions. Furthermore, since Groveland was a segregated lower-middle-class community, the involvement and interaction of the residents with whites and other ethnic groups were limited, and the adverse effects of prejudice and other racial indignities were thereby minimized. Finally, Groveland was not experiencing an inmigration of other ethnic groups. In fact, the combined population of whites, Latinos, and Asians was small and declining. Accordingly, institutions in Groveland were not only firmly controlled by African Americans, there was virtually no ethnic competition for public space and housing.

Yet the fact that ethnicity was not a factor in the day-to-day activities in Groveland did not remove anxieties about neighborhood change. The residents were concerned about the pressures from surrounding ghetto neighborhoods. As an attractive lower-middle-class community, Groveland enjoyed a quality of life that far exceeded that of the surrounding, less economically advantaged black communities. Families from nearby poor neighborhoods had begun to trickle in, and their behavior was carefully scrutinized. In block-club meetings residents expressed concern about the future of the neighborhood and what could happen if significant segments of the ghetto poor were able to gain a foothold in the community.[10]

In some respects, Groveland residents' expression of concern about the penetration of surrounding lower-class blacks into their neighborhood was not dissimilar to Beltway whites' apprehension about the entry of people of color into theirs. The fundamental difference, of course, was that the intergroup anxieties in Groveland represented class, not racial, antagonisms. Nonetheless, both neighborhoods were concerned about the impact of outside groups on community stability, and both neighborhoods feared lower-class populations. Although blacks in Groveland did not express their feelings about lower-class or ghetto blacks in racist terms, and although whites in Beltway were in many respects mixing race and class antagonisms in their sentiments about the penetration of outsiders, both communities were anxious about lower-income populations settling in their neighborhoods and concerned with issues raised by living in close proximity to poor people. Indeed, field notes compiled by our researchers revealed that the residents of each neighborhood expressed concerns about renters, who did not, in their judgment, share the values of homeowners.

Confronted with the options of exit and voice, Groveland residents seemed to be relying on the latter as they reacted to the behavior of recent residents, which sometimes challenged the traditions established by the older residents. Pressure was put on the new residents to conform to neighborhood standards. Loyalty to the neighborhood may play a significant role in this connection. A key factor in determining the future demographic makeup of Groveland is whether neighborhood loyalty will help reinforce voice and minimize exit if the in-migration from adjacent poor communities increases. What is clear, however, is that Groveland will remain racially segregated regardless of the class composition of the neighborhood. Whereas ethnic separation in the other three neighborhoods reflected a dynamic sifting process as different groups moved in and out, Groveland was unique in the sense that the in-migration was restricted to one group—African Americans.

THE RACIAL AND ETHNIC SEPARATION OF
NEIGHBORHOODS AND SOCIAL POLICY DILEMMAS

The findings of this research suggest several general principles that have implications for social policies in addressing the problems of racial and ethnic antagonism in large American metropolitan areas. In general, when residents perceive that in-migration presents a threat to their neighborhood, they will react either by exiting or by joining forces with other neighbors to resist the change. The stronger the social organization of the neighborhood, the more likely it is that local residents will select the voice option and take steps to keep the area stable. Residents are more likely to choose the exit option when they feel that a neighborhood's resources, including the social organization of the community, are insufficient to stem the tide of ethnic change.

The greater this feeling among residents, the more quickly the neighborhood reaches the "tipping point," the beginning of a very rapid ethnic turnover.[11] However, the literature on neighborhood racial or ethnic change does not provide a general set of arguments that relate the tipping point to neighborhood social organization, arguments that would help explain more fully why some neighborhoods reach the tipping point more rapidly than do others, or why some neighborhoods undergoing racial or ethnic change never reach the tipping point.[12]

The findings of this study suggest a positive relationship between the strength of neighborhood social organization and the length of time it takes to reach the tipping point after an ethnic invasion occurs. In our comparisons of Beltway and Dover, we highlighted the fact that Dover, unlike Beltway, had neither the institutional strength nor the population stability to prevent rapid ethnic turnover. Dover struggled through a period of economic decline in the 1970s, prior to the en masse in-migration of Mexicans, which resulted in significant out-migration of white residents, housing vacancies, and declining property values. The influx of Mexicans shored up the housing market in the 1980s. Nonetheless, by 1990 whites still constituted a substantial majority of the neighborhood's population. But weak neighborhood social organization—as reflected in public conflicts over the use of language, declining business and civic organizations, and cultural clashes between whites and Latinos in local churches—cleared the path for a rapid ethnic turnover. By contrast, Beltway had been a model of population and institutional stability until 1990. Although Beltway experienced some population movements in the 1990s, it remained a predominantly white community and continued to feature organizations that effectively resisted unwanted neighborhood change.

However, even with its relatively high level of social organization, in the 1990s Beltway experienced a notable decline in its white population, a significant rise in its Latino population, and small but symbolic increases in its Asian and black populations. Although whites still constituted more than three-quarters of the residents, the community was not nearly as ethnically homogeneous as it had been in previous years. The question remains: How long can the community prevent the neighborhood from reaching the dreaded tipping point?

Some communities with high levels of social organization and facing a modicum of penetration by outside ethnic groups have adopted "integration maintenance programs." Although such programs "are consistent with the spirit of residential desegregation," they actually violate the letter of the 1968 Fair Housing Act by limiting the housing options of racial minorities, either directly through quotas or indirectly through a series of procedures designed to control minority entry into the neighborhood.[13] In describing such programs, Douglas Massey and Nancy Denton state:

> Rather than seeking to change [the] discriminatory system of housing allocation, integration management programs accept it and seek to preserve a few islands of integration within a larger sea of racial exclusivity. Inevitably, many deserving black families with high aspirations for residential mobility are kept out so that a few privileged whites and blacks can enjoy the benefits of an economically stable, integrated neighborhood.[14]

Whether a neighborhood adopts a program backed by the rhetoric of "meaningful" integration or, like Beltway, pursues other initiatives that make no pretense about promoting integration but rather seek simply to preserve the stability of the neighborhood—even if that means preserving segregation—the success of such undertakings depends on the level of neighborhood social organization. If the city of Chicago is any indication, only a small percentage of urban neighborhoods have the resources to resist a transformation once a significant ethnic or racial invasion begins. And, to repeat, the weaker the social organization of the neighborhood, the more rapid the ethnic transformation.

Two parallel themes emerge from this examination of the four neighborhoods. One is our exploration of what makes for a stable and strong community, which everyone wants. We've attempted to shed light on how exit, voice, and loyalty determine whether neighborhoods continue strong and relatively stable. Strong neighborhoods often remain so in opposition to other groups of people, and this is the parallel theme of our book. Together, these forces work against the notion of intergroup harmony and integration in neighborhoods, schools, and the overall society that underlies the U.S. ideal. In other words, strong neighborhoods and community identities are a double-edged sword. Efforts to develop and sustain strong communities like Beltway and Groveland create resources that can be used to prevent or impede unwanted neighborhood integration—whether it be racial, as in Beltway, or class-based, as in Groveland.

On the other hand, neighborhoods that feature a weak social organization, such as Dover, will see their residents confront an unwanted ethnic invasion not by resorting to voice to prevent or stem the tide, but by choosing to exit, as whites in Dover did following a Latino invasion. This will eventually create a tipping point, or a rapid ethnic/racial transformation of the neighborhood.

Although the immediate future of Beltway is uncertain, a few decades ago Groveland changed from white to African American and Archer Park shifted from white to Latino. At the time of our study, Dover had only recently undergone an ethnic turnover, from white to Latino. For the most part, these population transformations have generated incredible racial and ethnic tensions. However, once a neighborhood has been transformed ethnically and the prospects for further ethnic change are low, racial and ethnic tensions within the neighborhood subside. Groveland, and to a lesser extent Archer Park, are cases in point.

Nonetheless, since urban neighborhoods are divided racially, ethnically, and culturally, the potential for ethnic conflict in the larger city is always present because groups are far more likely to focus on their differences than on their commonalities. Although they may be comfortable in their own monolithic neighborhoods, and although many of their members work in integrated employment settings, these groups are likely to view one another as competitors for political, social, and cultural resources.

Meanwhile, national and international trends are fostering rapid immigration, especially from neighboring Latino countries. In many ways this immigration strengthens the nation, as immigrants revitalize urban neighborhoods and economies. In other ways, the flow of immigrants from these countries to American urban neighborhoods not only exacerbates tensions between Latinos and whites, but also between Latinos and blacks, especially when the former position themselves in opposition to low-income African Americans, as did the Latinos in Archer Park.

The influx of immigrants also means that more people are competing for a limited urban social-funding pie. That pie has been shrinking, and because huge tax cuts in the midst of war have contributed to a serious national budget crisis, it will continue to shrink for some time to come. Moreover, with minorities, notably Latinos, displacing whites as a growing share of the population, the implications for urban tax bases are profound. According to the Census Bureau, the median annual household income for Latinos in 2000 was about $14,000 less than that of white households.

With a declining tax base and the simultaneous loss of federal funds that began with the New Federalist policies, first introduced during the Reagan administration, municipalities have had trouble raising enough revenue to cover basic services, and some have even cut such services in order to avoid bankruptcy.[15] Although fiscal conditions in many cities improved significantly in the latter half of the 1990s, this brief period of economic progress was ended by the recession of 2001, followed by a jobless recovery.

The Bush administration's substantial reductions in federal aid to states have exacerbated the problems of providing basic services in cities reliant on state funds.[16] Because of these combined economic and political changes, many central cities and inner suburbs lack the fiscal means to address the concentrated problems of joblessness, family breakups, and failing public schools.[17] And given the current budget deficit—which continues to grow because large tax cuts for wealthy citizens have been combined with the allocation of billions of federal dollars to pay for the wars in Iraq and Afghanistan, the war against terror, and the rebuilding of Iraq's infrastructure—support for programs to revitalize cities will very likely garner even less support from policymakers.[18]

Urban residents need to work together to secure greater funds for domestic social priorities, and also to win the backing of suburban constituencies for the same. The crime and social disarray associated with low-income inner-city residents undermine support for cities among more affluent people, no matter where they live. Cities need leaders who can somehow persuade middle- and low-income residents of the metropolitan region to make common cause, to realize that their lives inevitably intersect.[19] Some clues for how to achieve a sense of commonality among diverse groups arise from our study.

We saw that white and Latino parents in Dover set aside their ethnic antagonisms when they saw the need to join forces to prevent the busing of their children to black inner-city neighborhoods. A more positive example can be found in Beltway. White and Latino parents worked with the parents of black children who were bused into Beltway schools to address the problem of an autocratic local school council. The positive interaction of younger white and Latino parents with African American parents in confronting the school council was not the result of greater ethnic tolerance. Rather, the situation was conducive to uniting the races because all shared a common concern—the education of their children.

Social psychological research on group interdependence reveals that when groups believe they need one another, they are able to overcome their prejudices and can join in programs that foster mutual interaction and cooperation. Moreover, when people from different groups come together, their perceptions and behaviors tend to change.[20] The implication of this research is that urban leaders, especially political leaders, should work to make residents aware of their common needs and interests and thereby create a sense of interdependence that would facilitate collective political action to improve conditions in urban areas, including the quality of life.

This is a challenge. As long as groups are sorted into ethnically and racially monolithic neighborhoods, they are more likely to highlight group differences rather than commonalities, and are therefore less likely to see the need and appreciate the potential for mutual political support across racial and ethnic lines. That is why it is so important to create an atmosphere of local coalition-building that would bring together diverse communities to identify common goals and concerns shared by various groups.[21] We believe that goals specifying the improvement of public schools, expanded libraries, better parks, cleaner playgrounds, more efficient public transportation, and more reliable community services ranging from street cleaning to garbage collection could provide the common ground on which many diverse groups could meet.

Ideally, if local coalitions could then be expanded to form a multiracial national coalition, the political muscle needed to apply pressure for greater federal support for cities could be generated. Beginning in 1980, sharp spending cuts on direct aid to cities have included general revenue sharing, urban mass transit, economic development assistance, urban development action grants, social-service block grants, local public works, compensatory education, and public-service jobs and job training.[22] The federal contribution to city budgets was 17.5 percent in 1977; by 2000 it had dropped to 5.4 percent.[23] Furthermore, as noted previously, federal aid to states under the Bush administration has been substantially reduced, thereby aggravating the problems of providing basic services in cities that rely on state funds.[24]

With federal support, a more vibrant central city could

experience decreased social tensions and the reduction of ethnic competition associated with the desire to control shrinking resources. Moreover, increased federal support to cities could be used to help revitalize inner-city ghetto areas, and the sources of crime and other social dislocations could be mitigated.

Indeed, if there was a common concern among the residents of all four neighborhoods, it was the prevalence of crime and other social dislocations in nearby black ghetto neighborhoods. We cannot continue to ignore the needs of inner-city ghetto residents because these problems will not go away. If unaddressed, they may worsen, further driving middle-class people—including middle-class blacks—to abandon central cities, and further heightening racial tensions in ethnic neighborhoods such as Beltway, Dover, and Archer Park, and class tensions in non-poor African American neighborhoods such as Groveland. Thus, underlying much of the racial and class tensions in urban areas is the unresolved question of how to address the needs of low-income urban black residents.

The problems of social dislocation in inner-city ghettos—including poverty, joblessness, failing schools, and family breakups—are so massive that they require federal support on a significant scale if they are to be meaningfully addressed. One of the challenges facing efforts to achieve effective multiracial coalition building is mustering sufficient political pressure to revive funding for cities so that resources would be available to attack these problems.

However, if one of the explicit aims is to ameliorate problems in inner-city black ghettos, there are two major and related obstacles to overcome. The first is the general belief—prominently held by white and black conservatives—that racism is no longer an issue in this country;[25] the second is that government programs directed at improving conditions of people of color, including African Americans, are no longer warranted. Underlying both views is the following belief: if individual minorities are not succeeding today, it is due in large measure to their own shortcomings or inadequacies, not to lack of opportunity or to racism in the larger society. It is reasonable to assume that both views help to explain why white Americans overwhelmingly object to government assistance targeted at blacks. Today, whereas eight out of every ten African Americans feel that the government is not spending enough to assist black people, only slightly more than three of every ten white Americans feel this way.

The idea that the federal government "has a special obligation to help improve the living standards of blacks" because they "have been discriminated against for so long" was supported by only one in five whites in 2001, and has never exceeded more than one in four since 1975. Significantly, the lack of white support for this idea is not related to background factors such as level of education and age.

How much of this opposition to government assistance can be attributed to stereotypes about the cultural traits of blacks, including attitudes, orientations, worldviews, habits, and behavioral styles? In other words, how much of the opposition takes the form of racial ideology that Lawrence Bobo and his colleagues refer to as "laissez-faire racism," a racism in which blacks are perceived as being responsible for their own economic predicament and therefore undeserving of special government support?[26] In this connection, James Kluegel's study of trends in white explanations of the black-white economic gap provides persuasive testimony to continued racial stereotyping: between 1977 and 1989, the most frequently expressed reason for the economic gap was lack of motivation on the part of African Americans.[27] Such attitudes lead one to overlook the devastating cumulative effects of problems such as failing public schools that service children in inner-city ghetto neighborhoods and employer discrimination that continues to exacerbate the employment woes of low-income adult blacks, especially black males.[28]

Accordingly, if one of the aims is to address conditions in inner-city ghettos, coalition leaders will have to take into account the underlying and persistent laissez-faire racism that is prevalent today. In doing so, the issues would have to be framed in such a way that government programs for cities would be seen as benefiting all segments of the urban population—whites, African Americans, Latinos, Asians, and Native Americans. This doesn't mean that special programs would not be targeted at improving life in inner-city ghetto neighborhoods—such as public-service jobs and job training, economic development assistance, and neighborhood revitalization—but rather that such programs would be part of a more comprehensive package of reforms. Programs designed to improve the overall quality of life in the larger city would include those that are targeted at specific neighborhoods, including inner-city ghetto neighborhoods.

The American ideal of integrated neighborhoods may not be achieved for all the reasons stated in this book, but coalition-building would at least have the potential to create a sense of group interdependence, reduce racial and ethnic conflict, and enable diverse groups to live side by side in harmony, not fear.

A COMPARATIVE STUDY OF NEIGHBORHOODS
USING THE ETHNOGRAPHIC METHOD

The data presented in this study are based on two and a half years of field research, as well as on archival and historical research and the analysis of census statistics. The field research featured the ethnographic mode of empirical investigation in each of the four neighborhoods, including participant observation in multiple settings such as community-wide meetings (e.g., local school council meetings and meetings of the Ward Regular Democratic Organization), block-club meetings; local church meetings; other neighborhood activities and events; and casual conversations and interactions with neighborhood residents, as well as with those who worked there. The historical and archival research included the reading of books, newspapers, neighborhood flyers, photographs, and other documents on institutions and activities in the neighborhoods. Finally, the analysis of census data was used to gauge changes in the demographic characteristics of each neighborhood, as well as demographic changes in the city of Chicago.

The ethnographic research, the main source of data for this study, was conducted between January 1993 and September 1995. Although the field of sociology is replete with studies of individual neighborhoods using ethnographic research methods, this is the first time, to our knowledge, that social scientists have systematically used ethnographic methods to conduct a comparative community study—that is, to study several neighborhoods at the same time, collecting comparable data for analysis.

Armed with a set of guidelines, sociology graduate students at the University of Chicago entered these communities as observers, mapping key locations, conducting interviews, meeting with individuals informally, and in many cases providing volunteer services. Our ethnographic team consisted of nine University of Chicago graduate-student research assistants. Beltway, Dover, and Groveland each had two students, one male and one female, conducting fieldwork. We were able to match the races of the graduate students and the residents in Beltway and Groveland. Although the neighborhoods of Dover and Archer Park included substantial numbers of Latinos, we were unable to find graduate students of Latin American ethnicity to work on the project. However, all of the researchers assigned to these neighborhoods spoke at least some Spanish, and two of the field researchers in Archer Park were fluent in Spanish.

There are advantages and disadvantages to having the researchers and the subjects be of the same race and ethnicity; there are also advantages and disadvantages to having researchers with racial or ethnic backgrounds that differ from those of their subjects. For example, it is widely conceded that white scholars conducted two of the best ethnographic studies of African American neighborhoods.[1] Sometimes people will share information with ethnic outsiders that they would not impart to friends or coworkers. Why? Because the informant believes that the ethnic outsider is less likely to pass on confidential information to the informant's networks of relationships that he or she would not like to be revealed. Also, ethnic outsiders tend not to be influenced by the cultural constraints affecting ethnic insiders, constraints that may lead one to overlook or underestimate important patterns of behavior that are taken for granted by ethnic insiders. In other words, ethnic outsiders tend to observe behavior or action with fresh eyes.

On the other hand, there are implicit cultural meanings to behaviors that ethnic outsiders probably do not perceive. To the extent that there are barriers between ethnic insiders and outsiders, outsiders may have great difficulty gaining trust. In our study, the researchers working in the black community of Groveland and the white community of Beltway were relative insiders, and were more or less perceived by the residents as insiders. This facilitated their efforts to establish rapport with the residents. At the same time, the "outsider" researchers in Archer Park and Dover did, in fact, gain the trust and respect of both the Latino and white residents in these neighborhoods, and they were remarkably resourceful in making contacts and building ties.

The first several months of fieldwork were devoted to mapping and taking pictures in each neighborhood and to describing the institutional resources base, including businesses, parks, playgrounds, churches, housing stock, and public libraries. The field researchers also observed the casual interactions of residents in public spaces. Following these straightforward observations, a period of time was devoted to locating knowledgeable informants in each neighborhood, including aldermen, ministers and other church officials, school principals, police officials, librarians, directors of social welfare agencies, editors of neighborhood newspapers, and heads of community and local business organizations. Interviews with these individuals were conducted throughout the period of field research. Furthermore, a good deal of time was spent on establishing personal contacts and interacting with residents in each neighborhood. Finally, the field-workers in each neighborhood volunteered their time in community activities. These activities included jobs as a soccer coach, summer-camp counselor, choir conductor at a church, dance teacher at a school, and tutors at schools and public parks.

As the researchers established rapport with individuals and attended various local events, they wrote detailed field notes about their experiences, observations, and conversations. Each field-worker met twice a month with the two principal investigators (William Julius Wilson and Richard P. Taub) to discuss issues raised in his or her field notes and to ensure that comparable matters were being investigated in each neighborhood. For example, we pursued comparable questions on how residents understood and viewed such matters in their neighborhood as crime, gangs, neighborhood upkeep, racial and ethnic change, and the behavior of adolescents, as well as how these issues ought to be addressed.

Our research on neighborhood churches and schools provides two other examples. Since all public elementary and high schools in Chicago required that school councils consist of elected representatives chosen from among parents, community members, and teachers, we were interested in the extent to which council meetings varied by neighborhood. We therefore addressed questions concerning the role of the parents, the extent to which they were actively engaged in the meetings, and the kinds of issues they considered or pursued. We also examined questions about the roles of the principals in the various schools. The comparative questions concerning churches included the levels of resident participation in religious organizations and how religious leaders saw their roles and positions in terms of community concerns.

The merits of field (ethnographic) research, as compared to survey research and other modes of data collection that rely more heavily on statistics, have been extensively debated among social scientists. Unlike surveys, ethnographic research enjoys the advantage of protracted interactions or conversations over longer periods of time. People are able to provide detailed responses to questions and elaborate on complicated ideas without being restricted to the simplified forced-choice categories of most surveys.

Furthermore, in ethnographic field research the investigator has the opportunity to compare what people say they do with what they actually do, and can observe processes and sequences of events that produce outcomes—something not easy to capture with surveys. On the other hand, ethnographic field research has some limitations. There is the problem of sampling: the number of people the ethnographer encounters is relatively small, and may not be representative of the larger population. It is important that the research be guided by theoretical assumptions so that judgments can be made as to the extent to which the observations are consistent with the theoretical arguments. The selection of samples and the interpretation of findings are therefore based on their theoretical significance, not on the extent to which they represent a larger population in a statistical sense. Moreover, the ethnographic sample may not provide a true reflection of the distribution of attributes under consideration. Thus, in this study we turned to census data to provide averages or ranges of the distribution of attributes—such as neighborhood income, levels and types of occupation, etc.—as presented in Appendix B.

APPENDIX B

TABLE 1. SOCIOECONOMIC CHARACTERISTICS OF FOUR CHICAGO NEIGHBORHOODS, 1970–2000

	BELTWAY	DOVER	ARCHER PARK	GROVE-LAND
TOTAL POPULATION				
1970	24,488	35,618	62,895	14,412
1980	22,584	30,770	75,204	13,792
1990	21,490	32,207	81,155	11,711
2000	22,331	44,912	91,071	11,147
FAMILY DATA: % FAMILIES THAT ARE MARRIED COUPLES				
1970	89	81	79	81
1980	85	77	74	64
1990	78	68	69	55
2000	73	69	68	50
FAMILY DATA: % FAMILIES THAT ARE FEMALE-HEADED				
1970	8	14	15	15
1980	12	18	17	31
1990	16	23	19	38
2000	19	19	19	42
MEDIAN FAMILY INCOME[1]				
1969	—	—	—	—
1979	$53,551	$43,622	$34,905	$51,495
1989	$51,295	$39,814	$30,187	$51,568
1999	$54,037	$38,561	$32,317	$52,745

[1]Median incomes for 1979 and 1989 are presented in 1999 dollars. The adjustments for 1979 and 1989 are calculated using the revised CPI-U-RS series released in April 2002. Median income for 1969 is not presented, since the CPI-U-RS series is not available prior to 1978.

Appendix B

TABLE 1 *(continued)*

	BELTWAY	DOVER	ARCHER PARK	GROVE-LAND
% FAMILIES BELOW POVERTY LEVEL				
1969	3	6	12	5
1979	4	8	19	10
1989	3	10	22	12
1999	6	15	24	8
% ADULTS AGES 25+ WITH HIGH SCHOOL DIPLOMA OR HIGHER				
1970	46	34	27	60
1980	57	48	27	70
1990	70	53	31	78
2000	77	47	37	80
% ADULTS AGES 25+ WITH MORE THAN HIGH SCHOOL DIPLOMA				
1970	10	8	7	32
1980	16	15	9	39
1990	31	23	14	52
2000	39	21	18	58
% CIVILIAN LABOR FORCE AGES 16+ UNEMPLOYED				
1970	3	4	4	4
1980	6	8	14	9
1990	6	9	14	12
2000	5	12	12	8

Appendix B

	BELTWAY	DOVER	ARCHER PARK	GROVE-LAND
% CIVILIAN LABOR FORCE AGES 16+ WORKING IN WHITE-COLLAR JOBS				
1970	18	14	12	26
1980	47	45	26	59
1990	53	44	26	65
2000	54	36	28	65
% CIVILIAN LABOR FORCE AGES 16+ EMPLOYED BY GOVERNMENT				
1970	10	8	7	29
1980	14	10	7	31
1990	16	9	5	31
2000	21	7	6	27
% OWNER-OCCUPIED HOUSING UNITS				
1970	71	45	35	69
1980	70	49	37	73
1990	73	51	37	75
2000	74	51	36	74

TABLE 1 *(continued)*

	BELTWAY	DOVER	ARCHER PARK	GROVE-LAND
% PERSONS AGES 5+ LIVING IN THE SAME HOME IN 1965, 1975, 1985, 1995[2]				
1970	—	—	—	—
1980	65	63	46	77
1990	68	56	54	77
2000	62	52	55	77
MEDIAN HOUSE VALUE				
1970	$21,900	$16,800	$12,600	$19,900
1980	$54,100	$34,300	$27,700	$38,400
1990	$83,384	$57,445	$48,552	$65,881
2000	$132,280	$108,381	$105,201	$96,151

[2]1970 data is not presented, as it is not consistent with later census definitions.

Sources:

For 2000: Calculations based on data from Census 2000 Summary File (SF1) 100 Percent Data; Census 2000 Summary File (SF3); Northeastern Illinois Planning Commission, http://www.nipc.org/test/dp234_CA_2000htm#electronic.

For 1990: Calculations based on data from Census 1990 Summary Tape File 1 (SF1) 100 Percent Data; Census 1990 Summary File (SF3); The Chicago Fact Book Consortium, *Local Community Fact Book: Chicago Metropolitan Area, 1990* (Chicago: Academy Chicago Publishers, 1995); Northeastern Illinois Planning Commission, unpublished tables.

For 1980: Calculations based on data from Census 1980 Summary Tape File 1 (SF1) 100 Percent Data; 1980 Summary File (SF3); The Chicago Fact Book Consortium, *Local Community Fact Book: Chicago Metropolitan Area, 1980* (Chicago: Chicago Review Press, 1984); Northeastern Illinois Planning Commission, unpublished tables.

For 1970: Calculations based on data from U.S. Bureau of the Census, *1970 Census of Population and Housing: Census Tracts* (Washington, D.C.: U.S. Government Printing Office, 1972).

Appendix B

TABLE 2. OCCUPATIONAL DISTRIBUTION FOR THE EMPLOYED CIVILIAN POPULATION (16 YEARS AND OLDER) IN FOUR CHICAGO NEIGHBORHOODS, 2000

OCCUPATIONAL CATEGORIES	BELTWAY	DOVER	ARCHER PARK	GROVE-LAND
Professional, Managers, and Related Occupations	21%	11%	10%	32%
Service Occupations	19%	16%	18%	15%
Sales and Office Occupations	33%	24%	18%	33%
Farming, Fishing, and Forestry	0%	0%	0%	0%
Construction, Extraction, and Maintenance Occupations	9%	13%	12%	7%
Production, Transportation, and Material Moving Occupations	17%	35%	42%	13%

Source: Calculations based on Census 2000 data (SF3), Table DP-3, for Chicago Community Areas (tabulated by the Northeastern Illinois Planning Commission), http://www.nipc.org/test/dp234_CA_2000.htm#electronic.

Appendix B

TABLE 3. DISTRIBUTION OF GOVERNMENT WORKFORCE*
FOR THE EMPLOYED CIVILIAN POPULATION
(16 YEARS AND OLDER) IN FOUR CHICAGO
NEIGHBORHOODS, 1980–2000

	BELTWAY	DOVER	ARCHER PARK	GROVE-LAND
2000				
Civilian labor force employed by the government	21%	7%	6%	27%
Federal	2%	2%	1%	6%
State	1%	1%	1%	4%
Municipal	18%	5%	4%	17%
1990				
Civilian labor force employed by the government	16%	9%	5%	31%
Federal	1%	1%	1%	9%
State	2%	2%	1%	4%
Municipal	13%	6%	3%	19%
1980				
Civilian labor force employed by the government	14%	10%	7%	31%
Federal	2%	2%	1%	9%
State	1%	1%	1%	5%
Municipal	11%	7%	4%	17%

*Percentages of federal, state, and municipal workers may not always equal the total percentage of civilian labor force employed by the government due to rounding.

Sources:

For 2000: Calculations based on Census 2000 Summary File (SF3), Table P51.

For 1990: Calculations based on data from The Chicago Fact Book Consortium, *Local Community Fact Book: Chicago Metropolitan Area, 1990* (Chicago: Academy Chicago Publishers, 1995).

For 1980: Calculations based on data from The Chicago Fact Book Consortium, *Local Community Fact Book: Chicago Metropolitan Area, 1980* (Chicago: Chicago Review Press, 1984).

NOTES

CHAPTER ONE

1. The racial category "whites," as used in this book, refers to the census classification of "non-Hispanic whites." Census questions prior to 2000 allowed respondents to self-identify their race as White, Black, Native American, Asian or Pacific Islander, or Other. A follow-up question then asked respondents if they were of Hispanic ethnicity. The most recent census included an additional option for the race question, which allowed respondents to self-identify as bi- or multiracial. In previous years, these latter groups would have been counted in one of the single race categories. Therefore, population totals by race for 1980 and 1990 are not directly comparable to those for 2000. For the 2000 population figures presented in this book, respondents of Hispanic origin can be of any race, including those using the new multiracial category. The other racial categories, such as Non-Hispanic White, refer to people who classify themselves as being of only one race and not of Hispanic origin. In this book, the word "Latino" is used when referring to a person described in the census as Hispanic.

2. To further protect the identity of these four neighborhoods, we also use pseudonyms for the names of localities that border them, as well as for the names of streets, schools, churches, playgrounds, and other marks of identification within each neighborhood. Moreover, the names of the residents of these

neighborhoods who are quoted in this book also appear as pseudonyms. Finally, in several instances, where the name of a person or place is mentioned in direct quotes, we substitute the pseudonym in brackets.

The neighborhoods in our study represent four of Chicago's seventy-seven "community areas." A community area includes a number of adjacent census tracts.

3. David Willer, *Scientific Sociology: Theory and Method* (Englewood Cliffs, N.J.: Prentice Hall, 1967).

4. Albert O. Hirschman, *Exit, Voice, and Loyalty: Responses to Decline in Firms, Organizations, and States* (Cambridge: Harvard University Press, 1970).

5. Louis Rose, *The South Side: The Racial Transformation of an American Neighborhood* (Chicago: Ivan R. Dee, 1998); and John T. McGreevy, *Parish Boundaries: The Catholic Encounter with Race in the Twentieth-Century Urban North* (Chicago: University of Chicago Press, 1996).

6. Thomas C. Schelling, "Dynamic Models of Segregation," *Journal of Mathematical Sociology* 1 (1971): 143–86; Thomas C. Shelling, *Micromotives and Macrobehavior* (New York: Norton, 1978), pp. 135–66; Richard P. Taub, D. Garth Taylor, and Jan D. Durham, *Paths of Neighborhood Change: Race and Crime in Urban America* (Chicago: University of Chicago Press, 1984); William A. V. Clark, "Residential Preferences and Neighborhood Racial Segregation: A Test of the Schelling Segregation Model," *Demography* 28 (1991): 1–19; and John Yinger, *Closed Doors, Opportunities Lost: The Continuing Costs of Housing Discrimination* (New York: Russell Sage Foundation, 1995).

7. Hirschman, *Exit, Voice, and Loyalty,* p. 30.

8. Ibid., p. 51.

9. Hubert M. Blalock, *Toward a Theory of Minority-Group Relations* (New York: John Wiley & Sons, 1967). Recent research indicates that residential segregation has declined since 1970 mainly for non-poor families. On the other hand, poor black

families remain uniquely segregated. See Mary J. Fischer, "The Relative Importance of Income and Race in Determining Residential Outcomes in U.S. Urban Areas," *Urban Affairs Review* 38, no. 5 (May 2001): 669–96. Also see Ingrid Gould Ellen, *Sharing America's Neighborhoods: The Prospects for Stable Racial Integration* (Cambridge: Harvard University Press, 2000).

10. Blalock, *Toward a Theory of Minority-Group Relations.*

11. Hirschman, *Exit, Voice, and Loyalty.*

12. Ulf Hannerz, *Soulside: Inquiries into Ghetto Culture and Community* (New York: Columbia University Press, 1969); and Ann Swidler, "Culture in Action: Symbols and Strategies," *American Sociological Review* 51 (January 1986): 273–86. Also see Gerald Suttles, "The Cumulative Texture of Local Urban Culture," *American Journal of Sociology* 90 (1984): 283–302; and Albert Hunter, *Symbolic Communities* (Chicago: University of Chicago Press, 1978).

13. Robert J. Sampson and Walter Groves, "Community Structure and Crime: Testing Social-Disorganization Theory," *American Journal of Sociology* 94 (1989): 774–802.

14. Ibid. Also see Robert J. Sampson and William Julius Wilson, "Toward a Theory of Race, Crime, and Urban Inequality," in *Crime and Inequality,* ed. John Hagan and Ruth Peterson (Stanford: Stanford University Press, 1995), pp. 37–54.

15. Wall Street upgraded the ratings for bonds issued to finance infrastructure and other capital improvements during this period, a clear reflection of cities' improved fiscal outlook. Better bond ratings enable cities to pay investors lower interest rates, freeing up millions of dollars for vital services such as schools and even for cutting taxes for businesses and residents (U.S. Department of Housing and Urban Development, 1999).

16. Iris J. Lav and Andrew Brecher, "Passing Down the Deficit: Federal Policies Contribute to the Severity of the State Fiscal Crisis" (Center on Budget and Policy Priorities, Washington, D.C., May 12, 2004).

17. Bruce Katz, "Beyond City Limits: The Emergence of a New Metropolitan Agenda," unpublished ms. (Brookings Institution, Washington, D.C., April 1999), p. 1.

CHAPTER TWO

1. In 2000, 21 percent of the employed population in Beltway indicated that they were government employees, including 18 percent who worked for the city as police officers, firefighters, park employees, and streets and sanitation workers (see Table 1, Appendix B).

2. For a more detailed discussion of the feelings of Beltway residents about their neighborhood, see the study of one of our collaborators, Maria Kefalas, *Working-Class Heroes: Protecting Home, Community, and Nation in a Chicago Neighborhood* (Berkeley: University of California Press, 2003).

3. Ron Grossman and Charles Leroux, "A Local Outpost of Democracy," *Chicago Tribune,* March 5, 1996, pp. 1, 11.

4. The 1988 School Reform Act, which aimed to improve Chicago public schools, established local school councils to give parents and other community interests a decision-making role. Councils for elementary schools include the principal and parent, community, and teacher representatives. High school councils also include a student representative who votes on a limited number of issues.

5. Christopher Lasch, *The True and Only Heaven: Progress and Its Critics* (New York: Norton, 1991), p. 490. See also Michèle Lamont, *The Dignity of Working Men: Morality and the Boundaries of Race, Class, and Immigration* (Cambridge: Harvard University Press, 2000).

6. Lasch, *The True and Only Heaven.*

7. The joint efforts of veterans' organizations throughout the country were successful, as the U.S. Postal Service introduced the POW/MIA stamp on May 29, 1995 (Memorial Day).

8. See Wesley G. Skogan, *Disorder and Decline: Crime and the Spiral of Decay in American Neighborhoods* (New York: Free Press, 1990).
9. For a discussion of homes and ownership in Beltway, see Kefalas, *Working-Class Heroes.*
10. Our field-workers felt that the police officer clearly intended to elicit an emotional response, perhaps to garner support for more police funding.
11. Albert O. Hirschman, *Exit, Voice, and Loyalty: Responses to Decline in Firms, Organizations, and States* (Cambridge: Harvard University Press, 1970).

CHAPTER THREE

1. While there is widespread consensus among longtime Dover residents that the community is much less cohesive than it once was, care must be taken not to overly romanticize the past. Residents usually describe a close-knit community with limits; people knew everyone on their street but did not necessarily associate with people from all parts of the neighborhood. Some residents also complained that when Dover was virtually all white, the residents never built a large community center or a YMCA. Chicago city records indicate that of all the neighborhoods in Chicago, Dover is one of the community areas with the least amount of public space devoted to recreation and park facilities. See Melaniphy and Associates, "Citywide Findings and Conclusions: Chicago Comprehensive Neighborhood Needs Analysis Project," submitted to the honorable Jane M. Byrne (Chicago: Melaniphy and Associates, 1982).
2. Calculations for English-language proficiency based on data for Chicago community areas released by the Northeastern Illinois Planning Commission, 2002: http://www.nipc.org/test/dp234_CA_2000htm#electronic.
3. According to the 1990 census, the Chicago metropolitan area

was home to nearly 900,000 Polish immigrants. Much is made of the fact that Chicago has the second-largest concentration of Poles in the world; only Warsaw, Poland's capital, exceeds it.

4. Samuel H. Preston, "Children and the Elderly: Divergent Paths for America's Dependents," *Demography* 21 (1984): 435–57.

5. For further elaboration on these conceptual distinctions applied to Dover, see one of the collaborators of our study, Chenoa Flippen, "Neighborhood Transition and Social Organization: The White to Hispanic Case," *Social Problems* 48, no. 3 (2001): 299–321.

6. In 2000, 43 percent of Latinos age twenty-five and older in Dover had less than a ninth-grade education, compared with 10 percent of whites, 15 percent of blacks, and 17 percent of Asians. Moreover, 63 percent of Latino adults had not graduated from high school, compared with 32 percent of whites, 35 percent of blacks, and 29 percent of Asians. These calculations are based on the U.S. Bureau of the Census, 2000 Summary File (SF3).

7. The only references school officials made concerned gang violence, which they considered primarily territorial rather than ethnic, or between blacks and Latinos.

8. This trend may also reflect the fact that high school dropout rates, especially in urban schools, result in senior classes that are significantly smaller than freshman classes. Nonetheless, the magnitude of the disparity between the number of freshmen and the number of seniors suggest that increased enrollments largely accounted for the difference.

9. Translated from Spanish.

10. At the time we conducted our research, black children at the local magnet school no longer participated in athletic activities at the local park because of incidents of verbal intimidation. As the principal of the local magnet school put it, "We didn't feel it was a good environment for our kids . . . to be in. We were targeted because we were the only . . . ones with African Americans in our school." Residents on the street described the violence

and intimidation used against African Americans who tried to move into the neighborhood. Asked about blacks in the neighborhood, three men in their late fifties—two white and one Latino—responded that no blacks resided in the area because they did not want to move in. The men indicated that one black family had lived in the neighborhood many years ago, but when the mother and father died, their children sold the property. The men also mentioned that a black family had moved in ten years ago, but despite efforts by police to protect them, Mexicans ran them out.

CHAPTER FOUR

1. These calculations are based on data for Chicago community areas released by the Northeastern Illinois Planning Commission in 2002. See http://www.nipc.org/test/dp234_CA_2000 .htm#electronic.
2. George Rosen, *Decision-Making Chicago-Style: The Genesis of a University of Illinois Campus* (Urbana: University of Illinois Press, 1980).
3. U.S. Bureau of the Census, 2000 Summary File (SF3).
4. Of course, the idea that all European immigrants intended to remain in the United States is exaggerated. Recent research shows that many workers intended to work for a period of time and then return to their homes; thus, many never brought their wives and children to America. As many as three to four million Europeans actually did return to their home countries after working in the United States. See Mark Wyman, *Round-Trip to America: The Immigrants Return to Europe, 1880–1930* (Ithaca: Cornell University Press, 1993).
5. David M. Kennedy, *Freedom from Fear: The American People in Depression and War, 1929–1945* (New York: Oxford University Press, 1999).
6. *Community Area Book* (Chicago: Chicago Association of Commerce, 1970); *Demographic Characteristics of Chicago's Popula-*

tion (Chicago: City of Chicago, Department of Planning and Development, 1980); Census Bureau 2000 data from the SF1 data set; and Northeastern Illinois Planning Commission, 2002: http://www.nipc.org/test/dp234_CA_2000.htm#electronic.

7. See Table 1, Appendix B.

8. *Community Area Book* (1970), and U.S. Bureau of the Census, 2000 Summary File (SF3). See also Table 1, Appendix B.

9. "When Politics Trumps Education," op-ed, *Chicago Tribune,* August 22, 2001, p. 21.

10. Another possible explanation for the absence of protest over busing is that the residents of Archer Park do not tend to organize outside of kinship, and the protests in Dover depended greatly on the presence of the white protest leadership—and the main leadership was white—who had learned the language and modes of racial/ethnic protest via historical experience with, most notably, the civil rights era.

11. Private communication, July 11, 2002.

12. See Herbert Blumer, "Race Prejudice as a Sense of Group Position," *Pacific Sociological Review* 1 (Spring 1958): 3–7. For a more recent view, see Joe Feagin, Hernan Vera, and Pinar Batur, *White Racism,* 2nd ed. (New York: Routledge, 2001).

13. In addition to making intra-Mexican distinctions, Archer Park Mexicans disassociate themselves from Puerto Ricans. Although Puerto Ricans compose only 1 percent of the neighborhood, they are poorer than Mexicans, and many Archer Park Mexicans characterize Puerto Ricans as a group apart—people who are less refined. For example, Mexicans employed at an auto body shop just outside Archer Park called Puerto Ricans "stupid, lazy, and dirty," and added that they would never choose to live close to Puerto Ricans. A principal of a local elementary school who spoke Puerto Rican Spanish attested that Mexicans in the community had not accepted her at first. Mexican high school students also made pejorative jokes about Puerto Rican customs and fought repeatedly with Puerto Rican students. See North-

eastern Illinois Planning Commission: http://www.nipc.org/test/dp234_CA_2000.htm#electronic.

14. For two decades Statistical Policy Directive No. 15 of the Office of Management and Budget (OMB) provided guidelines for comparing data on race and ethnicity. Revised in October 1997, the new federal standards represent the government's view that people of Hispanic descent may be of any race.

15. Peter Skerry, *Mexican Americans: The Ambivalent Minority* (Cambridge: Harvard University Press, 1995). For an interesting account of how Mexicans view themselves as an immigrant group in Chicago, see William Kornblum, *Blue Collar Community* (Chicago: University of Chicago Press, 1974). See also Carola Suárez-Orozco and Marcelo Suárez-Orozco, "Migration: Generational Discontinuities and the Making of Latino Identities," in *Ethnic Identity: Creation, Conflict and Accommodation*, 3rd ed., ed. Lola Romanucci-Ross and George A. De Vos (Walnut Creek, Calif.: Altamira Press, 1995); and Frank D. Bean and Marta Tienda, *The Hispanic Population of the United States* (New York: Russell Sage, 1987), especially the chapter titled "The Structuring of Hispanic Ethnicity."

16. It could be argued that all four of our neighborhoods are "stepping-stone" communities. However, that designation is far more applicable to Archer Park. Unlike Beltway, Groveland, and Dover, the signs of transience permeated the neighborhood.

CHAPTER FIVE

1. For a more detailed discussion of the history of Groveland, see the study of one of our collaborators, Mary Pattillo-McCoy, *Black Picket Fences: Privilege and Peril Among the Black Middle Class* (Chicago: University of Chicago Press, 1999). We are indebted to her for some of the material in this section.

2. For a useful history of Chicago's Black Belt and numerous studies of its expansion through the decades, see Chapter 1 of Arnold R. Hirsch, *Making the Second Ghetto: Race and Housing*

in Chicago, 1940–1960 (Chicago: University of Chicago Press, 1983). In 1890 the Black Belt extended only from 22nd to 31st streets, but by 1940 it had expanded to 55th Street on the south and was bordered on the east and west by Cottage Grove and Wentworth avenues, respectively. See also St. Clair Drake and Horace Cayton, *Black Metropolis: A Study of Negro Life in a Northern City* (New York: Harcourt Brace Jovanovich, 1945; rev. ed., 1962); and Allan Spear, *Black Chicago: The Making of a Negro Ghetto, 1890–1920* (Chicago: University of Chicago Press, 1967).

3. Hirsch, *Making the Second Ghetto,* p. 46.
4. Northeastern Illinois Planning Commission, 2002: http://www.nipc.org/test/dp234_CA_2000.htm#electronic.
5. Residents of surrounding neighborhoods undergoing racial transformation mirrored the efforts of Groveland's new black homeowners. A resident of one of those neighborhoods recalled, "We were cautious in those days. I'd watch the man next door. I wanted to assure him that I was just as interested in maintaining property as he was. Every time he went to work on his grass, I went out to work on mine. I had nightmares about weeds." Quoted in Eduardo Camacho and Ben Joravsky, *Against the Tide: The Middle Class in Chicago* (Chicago: Community Renewal Society, 1989), p. 46.
6. William Julius Wilson, *When Work Disappears: The World of the New Urban Poor* (New York: Knopf, 1996). Also see Lawrence Katz, "Wage Subsidies for the Disadvantaged," Working Paper 5679 (Cambridge, Mass.: National Bureau of Economic Research, 1996).
7. This population loss does not reflect a decline in the community's quality of life, as demand for housing has remained fairly steady. The population loss probably reflects instead the aging of Groveland's population.
8. Marcus Garvey originated the red, black, and green flag during his pan-African movement of the early twentieth century.

9. Situated on Groveland's southern edge, Timberlin was built in the late 1950s and inhabited by Chicagoans who worked downtown, including a substantial Jewish population. Developed for relatively affluent professionals, Timberlin features suburban ranch-style houses that are larger than the traditional Chicago bungalows. Its winding streets often lead to dead ends, cordoning it off from the rest of the community.

10. See, for example, Ellis Cose, *The Rage of a Privileged Class* (New York: HarperCollins, 1993); and Ralph Wiley, *Why Black People Tend to Shout: Cold Facts and Wry Views from a Black Man's World* (New York: Penguin, 1991).

11. Black businesses face challenges in providing high-quality goods at low prices because of their smaller size and shallow pool of resources. African American business owners have been oppressed historically, through Jim Crow in the South and racial discrimination in the North. These experiences continue to affect perceptions of black and white businesses today, even when the quality of goods and services does not differ.

12. See Cose, *The Rage of a Privileged Class*.

13. See Table 3, Appendix B.

14. Mason was talking about a ban on FOR SALE signs in the 1960s that was designed at least partly to stop white flight. While perhaps well-intentioned, the result was the growth of a clandestine housing market that relied on personal networks and word of mouth. This lack of openness tended to keep houses in white neighborhoods in white hands, since people had few interracial social and professional contacts. This approach also encouraged racial "steering," in which real estate professionals guide homebuyers toward certain neighborhoods. In 1977 the Supreme Court found that municipalities and neighborhoods that banned FOR SALE signs violated First Amendment rights. Today such signs are common in Chicago's more affluent neighborhoods, including the rapidly growing Near West Side, the expanding South Loop, and the integrated, high-income com-

munity of Hyde Park/Kenwood. However, some sellers remain reluctant to advertise their homes to ensure that the "wrong people" do not buy into a community.

15. David O. Sears and John B. McConahay, *The Politics of Violence: The New Urban Blacks and the Watts Riot* (Boston: Houghton Mifflin, 1973); Castellano Turner and William Julius Wilson, "Dimensions of Racial Ideology: An Empirical Study of Urban Black Attitudes," *Journal of Social Issues* 32 (Spring 1976): 139–52; Gerald David Jaynes and Robin M. Williams, Jr., eds., Committee on the Status of Black Americans, Commission on Behavioral and Social Sciences and Education, National Research Council, *A Common Destiny: Blacks and American Society* (Washington, D.C.: National Academy Press, 1989).

16. See Signithia Fordham and John Ogbu, "Black Students' School Success: Coping with the Burden of 'Acting White,' " *Urban Review* 18, no. 3 (1986): 176–206.

17. For an interesting discussion of this point, see the study by one of our collaborators, Reuben A. Buford May, *Talking at Trena's: Everyday Conversation at an African American Tavern* (New York: New York University Press, 2001).

18. According to Colleen Lazar, associate director of international relations at the Chicago Mercantile Exchange, a runner is "an entry-level position on the trading floor, one of several types of trading-floor personnel employed by CME member firms (i.e., J.P. Morgan, Merrill Lynch) . . . A runner's primary responsibility is to deliver the customer order to the appropriate broker in the appropriate trading pit. Once the order has been filled, it is returned to the firm's trading desk for confirmation as soon as possible. However, actual running on the trading floor is strictly prohibited because it interferes with the flow of business. Runners must know the layout of the pits on the trading floor, as well as the names and locations of brokers in the pits who execute orders for their firm. A majority of the brokers working for firms began their work on the floor as runners." Private communication, May 2001.

19. See, for example, Derrick Bell, *Faces at the Bottom of the Well: The Permanence of Racism* (New York: BasicBooks, 1992); Cose, *The Rage of a Privileged Class;* and Joe R. Feagin and Melvin P. Sikes, *Living with Racism: The Black Middle-Class Experience* (Boston: Beacon, 1994).

20. See Table 1, Appendix B.

21. U.S. Bureau of the Census, 2000, from the SF3, Table P150B. See also Table 1, Appendix B.

22. Groveland residents generally feel that the U.S. Department of Housing and Urban Development's efforts to promote rent vouchers encourage landlords to cater to low-income residents.

23. Despite the presence of the gang, those who used the field house were generally well behaved, and it was always very clean. The pleasant conditions were due in no small measure to the gang leader, who wanted to keep things running smoothly to avoid attracting police attention.

24. Deborah Prothrow-Stith, *Deadly Consequences* (New York: HarperCollins, 1991); and Wilson, *When Work Disappears.*

CHAPTER SIX

1. Douglas S. Massey and Nancy A. Denton provide one of the most forceful and articulate arguments for this point of view. See *American Apartheid: Segregation and the Making of the Underclass* (Cambridge: Harvard University Press, 1993).

2. William Julius Wilson, *The Bridge over the Racial Divide: Rising Inequality and Coalition Politics* (Berkeley: University of California Press, 1999), p. 8. See also Harold P. Freeman, "Poverty, Race, Racism, and Survival," *Annals of Epidemiology* 3, no. 2 (1993): 145–49; and Harold Freeman, "The Meaning of Race in Science—Considerations for Cancer Research," *Cancer* 82, no. 1 (January 1, 1998): 219–25.

3. For further discussion of these and similar points, see Henry Allen Bullock, "Urbanism and Race Relations," in *The Urban South,* ed. Rupert B. Vance and Nicholas J. Demerath (Chapel

Hill: University of North Carolina Press, 1954), pp. 207–29; Ray Marshall, "Industrialisation and Race Relations in the Southern United States," in *Industrialisation and Race Relations: A Symposium,* ed. Guy Hunter (London: Oxford University Press, 1965), pp. 200–253; Hylan Lewis, "Innovations and Trends in the Contemporary Southern Negro Community," *Journal of Social Issues* 10 (1954): 22–24; and M. Elaine Burgess, "Race Relations and Social Change," in *The South in Continuity and Change,* ed. John C. McKinney and Edgar T. Thompson (Durham: Duke University Press, 1965), pp. 337–58.

4. William Julius Wilson, *The Declining Significance of Race: Blacks and Changing American Institutions* (Chicago: University of Chicago Press, 1980).

5. Albert O. Hirschman, *Exit, Voice, and Loyalty: Responses to Decline in Firms, Organizations, and States* (Cambridge: Harvard University Press, 1970)

6. See Table 3, Appendix B.

7. Hubert M. Blalock, *Toward a Theory of Minority-Group Relations* (New York: John Wiley & Sons, 1967).

8. See Table 1, Appendix B.

9. Ibid.

10. For a discussion of middle-class blacks' concerns about low-income blacks moving into their neighborhood in another Chicago community, see Richard P. Taub, D. Garth Taylor, and Jan D. Durham, *Paths of Neighborhood Change: Race and Crime in Urban America* (Chicago: University of Chicago Press, 1984).

11. Thomas C. Schelling, "Dynamic Models of Segregation," *Journal of Mathematical Sociology* 1 (1971): 143–86; Thomas C. Shelling, *Micromotives and Macrobehavior* (New York: Norton, 1978), pp. 135–66; Taub, Taylor, and Durham, *Paths of Neighborhood Change;* William A. V. Clark, "Residential Preferences and Neighborhood Racial Segregation: A Test of the Schelling Segregation Model," *Demography* 28 (1991): 1–19; and John Yinger, *Closed Doors, Opportunities Lost: The Continuing Costs of*

Housing Discrimination (New York: Russell Sage Foundation, 1995).

12. For a comprehensive discussion of this literature, see Ingrid Gould Ellen, *Sharing America's Neighborhoods: The Prospects for Stable Racial Integration* (Cambridge: Harvard University Press, 2000).

13. Massey and Denton, *American Apartheid,* p. 226.

14. Ibid., p. 227.

15. U.S. Department of Housing and Urban Development, *The State of Cities* (Washington, D.C.: U.S. Government Printing Office, 1999).

16. Iris J. Lav and Andrew Brecher, "Passing Down the Deficit: Federal Policies Contribute to the Severity of the State Fiscal Crisis" (Center on Budget and Policy Priorities, Washington, D.C., May 12, 2004).

17. Bruce Katz, "Beyond City Limits: The Emergence of a New Metropolitan Agenda," unpublished ms. (Brookings Institution, Washington, D.C., April 1999), p. 1.

18. Economists Linda Bilmes and Joseph E. Stiglitz estimate that the final bill for the Iraq war will be between $1 trillion and $2 trillion, depending on how much longer U.S. soldiers remain in Iraq. See Linda Bilmes and Joseph E. Stiglitz, "The Economic Costs of the Iraq War: An Appraisal Three Years After the Beginning of the Conflict," paper prepared for presentation at the annual meeting of the Allied Social Science Association, Boston, January 6–8, 2006.

19. There is growing evidence that cities and suburbs are economically interdependent. Recent research indicates that the higher the ratio of city to suburb per capita income, the higher the percentage of metropolitan employment growth and income growth, and the greater the increase in housing values; that improvements in central city capital stock also increase suburban housing values, suggesting that "suburban residents may have an incentive to increase contributions toward city infra-

structure"; that the reduction of central city poverty is associated with increases in metropolitan income growth; and that central city job growth increases the value of suburban properties. See Paul D. Gottlieb, *The Effects of Poverty on Metropolitan Area Economic Performance,* research report of the National League of Cities (June 1998).

20. See D. W. Johnson, R. Johnson, and G. Maruyama, "Goal Interdependence and Interpersonal Attraction in Heterogenous Classrooms: A Meta-Analysis," in *Groups in Contact: The Psychology of Desegregation,* ed. N. Miller and M. B. Brewer (Orlando: Academic Press, 1984), pp. 187–212. Also see Susan T. Fiske, "Stereotyping, Prejudice, and Discrimination," in *The Handbook of Social Psychology,* 4th ed., ed. D. T. Gilbert, S. T. Fiske, and G. Lindzey (New York: McGraw Hill, 1998).

21. Wilson, *The Bridge over the Racial Divide.* Also see Karen M. Kaufmann, "Cracks in the Rainbow: Group Commonality as a Basis for Coalition Between Latinos and African-Americans," *Political Research Quarterly* 56, no. 2 (June 2003): 199–210.

22. See Demetrios Caraley, "Washington Abandons the Cities," *Political Science Quarterly* 107 (Spring 1992): 1–30.

23. Bruce A. Wallin, "Budgeting for Basics: The Changing Landscape of City Finances," discussion paper prepared for the Brookings Institution Metropolitan Policy Program (Washington, D.C.: Brookings Institution, August 2005).

24. Lav and Brecher, "Passing Down the Deficit."

25. See, for example, Dinesh D'Souza, *The End of Racism: Principles for a Multiracial Society* (New York: Free Press, 1995); and Walter E. Williams, *More Liberty Means Less Government: Our Founders Knew This Well* (Stanford, Calif.: Hoover Institution, 1999).

26. See Lawrence Bobo and James R. Kluegel, "Status, Ideology, and Dimensions of Whites' Racial Beliefs and Attitudes: Progress and Stagnation," in *Racial Attitudes in the 1990s,* ed. Steven A.

Tuch and Jack K. Martin (Westport, Conn.: Praeger, 1997), pp. 93–120.

27. James R. Kluegel, "Trends in Whites' Explanations of the Gap in Black-White Socioeconomic Status, 1977–1989," *American Sociological Review* 55 (1990): 512–25.

28. Wilson, *When Work Disappears;* and Jean Anyon, *Ghetto Schooling: A Political Economy of Urban Educational Reform* (New York: Teachers College Press, 1997).

APPENDIX A

1. Elliot Liebow, *Tally's Corner: A Study of Negro Streetcorner Men* (Boston: Little, Brown, 1967); and Ulf Hannerz, *Soulside: Inquiries into Ghetto Culture and Community* (New York: Columbia University Press, 1969).

INDEX

ACCION International, 107, 109
ACORN, 107
Adamski, John, 20, 33
Afghanistan war, 183
African Americans, 3, 5, 11,
102–5, 115, 125, 128–60, 167,
172, 175–7, 181, 187, 188,
192, 203n1, 208n6; attitudes
toward whites of, 138–44;
businesses owned by, 213n11;
class distinctions among,
154–9, 164, 176, 186; in
community organizations, 106,
131–2; in competition for
public facilities, 116–18;
defining racial boundaries by,
148–54; discrimination
experienced by, 144–7; in
ethnically transitioning
neighborhood, 49, 54, 59,
61; as graduate student
investigators, 12; as
homeowners, 130–1; identity
of, 134–8, 158–9; Latino
antagonism toward, 90–3,
119–24, 127, 143, 165, 170,
173–4, 182, 208–9n10;
migration from South of, 128,
163; occupational status of,

132–3; political participation
of, 133–4; in predominantly
white community, 17, 46, 47,
179; religion of, 73–4; schools
and, 21–2, 30, 31, 77–85, 89,
114, 115, 160, 184, 208–9n10;
as taxpayers, 26; white flight
from, 128–9, 163–6
age differences, see generational
tensions
AIDS, 108
Alvarez, Jose, 88
AmeriCorps, 118
Archer Park, 4, 5, 12, 14, 81,
96–127, 137, 143, 171–5,
186, 210nn10, 13; anti-black
sentiment in, 119–24, 174,
182; community organizations
in, 105–9, 115–16;
competition for public
recreational space in, 116–19;
declining white population of,
98–102, 165, 171–2; fieldwork
conducted in, 192, 193;
government workforce in, 202;
growing Latino population in,
9–10, 17, 98, 102–4, 134;
language differences in,
99–100; occupational

· 221 ·

Index

diverse, 142–4, 146–7; *see also*
busing
Section 8 housing, 156
segregation, 180; de facto, 163–4;
Jim Crow, 145, 163, 213*n*11
Seneca, 113
Shelton, Ron, 149
Snipes, Wesley, 150
social class, *see* class differences
social organization, 11–12, 45,
126, 167–8, 178–81; belief
system and, 31–45, 168; class
and, 159–60; competition for
resources and, 116–19; race and,
27–31, 115–16; relative social
status and, 119–25
Social Security Administration,
143
social service providers, 108–9
South, migration to Chicago from,
128, 163
Southeast Side Home-Equity
Program, 144
"stepping-stone" communities,
125–7, 211*n*16
stereotypes, racial and ethnic, 31,
63; maintaining boundaries
through, 149–50; poverty and,
93, 120, 121, 187–8
Stiglitz, Joseph E., 217*n*18
Stockton, 77, 81, 89
Supreme Court, U.S., 28,
213*n*14

tax base, declining, 182–3
theoretical sampling, 5
tipping point, 7, 125, 178, 179,
181
Tubman, Harriet, 135

U.S. Army, 35
U.S. Postal Service, 34, 206*n*7

UNO, 107
Urban League, 153

Veterans Day, 33
Vietnam War, 34
violence, 121, 157; gang, *see* gangs;
in schools, 22; white flight and,
128–30
voice, *see* exit, voice, and loyalty,
theory of
voting: by African Americans, 134,
154; class and, 92–3; by Latinos,
88, 89, 96
Voting Rights Act, 153

Washington, Booker T., 135
Washington, Harold, 136
Wattleton, Faye, 135
Weston, 141
White Men Can't Jump (movie),
149–50
whites, 3–5, 14–96, 104–5, 134,
138, 153, 166–9, 176, 188,
203*n*1, 208*n*6, 209*n*10, 210*n*10;
African American attitudes
toward, 139–52, 175;
antagonism toward minorities
of, 23–7, 90–3, 187; arrival of
minorities seen as threat by,
18–21, 166–7; belief system of,
31–45; business and civic
organizations of, 65–70,
94–5; Catholic, 71–4; civil
rights movement and, 5–6;
declining population of, 48–52;
flight from desegregating
neighborhoods of, 6–10, 14, 19,
47, 95, 128–30, 146, 163–5; as
graduate student investigators,
12; and growing Latino
population, 10, 53–64, 93–4,
98–102, 113, 114, 116, 119,